GOD'S
DEVOTIONAL
BOOK
FOR MOTHERS

HONOR  BOOKS

Inspiration and Motivation for the Seasons of Life

An Imprint of Cook Communications Ministries • Colorado Springs, CO

GOD'S
DEVOTIONAL
BOOK
FOR MOTHERS

INTRODUCTION

Today's busy moms often have a problem: not enough time to read. *God's Devotional Book for Mothers* provides a good solution!

Each of the devotionals presented on the following pages can be read within a matter of a few minutes, yet each gives to the reader truth and inspiration to last all day. Each is based not only upon a positive and beneficial quotation, but also on a passage from God's Word. As such, these devotionals are not only timely, but timeless. Indeed, they each have an eternal spiritual truth embedded in them.

With moral training lacking in so many areas of our culture today, the stories and illustrations presented here provide a means for a woman to reinforce within herself what she knows to be good, right, and just. Many of the illustrations are ones a mother might share with her children, regardless of their ages.

The Word of God gives us the principle for acquiring God's truth in our lives: "For precept must be upon precept, precept upon precept; line upon line, line upon line; here a little, and there a little" (Isaiah 28:10). *God's Devotional Book for Mothers*—guaranteed to provide insight and inspiration to mothers everywhere!

SAFETY FIRST

> AS A **MOTHER,**
> MY JOB IS TO
> **TAKE CARE** OF THE
> POSSIBLE AND
> **TRUST** GOD WITH
> THE **IMPOSSIBLE.**
>
> RUTH BELL GRAHAM

DURING A LONG, winding drive through the Italian Alps, two-year-old Alexandra Chalupa slept safely buckled in her backseat car seat. When she awoke, she pleaded to be allowed to sit up front, snuggled between her parents. Tanya Chalupa said no to her toddler's further protests. Moments later, their car skidded in the rain, lurched across traffic lanes, barely missed a deep gorge, and came to rest against a solid wall of rock. Her parents were bruised and shaken, but Alexandra remained firmly fastened and unhurt. Tanya shuddered to think what would have happened if she had been holding her daughter in her lap.

After the family returned to California, Tanya began a one-woman campaign to enact legislation requiring automobile safety seats for children under four years old or weighing less than forty pounds. The memory of the accident and a conviction that such a law would save lives gave her the courage for a four-year campaign, even though she had no political know-how or financial backing. In 1983, the Child Restraint Law went into effect in California, and by year's end, child-passenger injuries had declined by more than four hundred from the previous year!

Those who know Your name will
put their trust in You; For You, LORD, have not
forsaken those who seek You.

PSALM 9:10 NKJV

TOP **10** TIPS

What the Bible Says You
Can Know and Do
Concerning Your Children

1. GOD BREATHED LIFE INTO YOUR CHILD AND KNOWS THE
NUMBER OF EVERY HAIR ON HIS OR HER HEAD.

2. GOD ALWAYS SEES YOUR CHILD.

3. GOD LOVES YOUR CHILD IMMEASURABLY MORE THAN YOU DO.

4. GOD CONSIDERS YOUR CHILD HIS OWN.

5. GOD WANTS THE VERY BEST FOR YOUR CHILD—
AND HE KNOWS WHAT IS THE "VERY BEST."

6. GOD URGES YOU TO PRAY FOR YOUR CHILD.

7. GOD PROMISES THAT WHEN YOU PRAY, HE IS LISTENING
AND TAKES YOUR REQUESTS TO HEART.

8. GOD HAS PROVIDED WISDOM
THROUGH THE HOLY SPIRIT.

9. GOD REMINDS YOU THAT ADVERSITY BUILDS
STRENGTH AND HE'S ABLE TO GIVE YOUR CHILD HELP
AND PEACE IN ANY CIRCUMSTANCE.

10. GOD URGES YOU TO LET GO OF ANXIETY ABOUT YOUR CHILD.

CONSIDER
THIS!

Is your home an open place?
Whether big or small,
Have you made a space
For friends, family
To respite for a time?
A day for a child to simply find
A place to exist safely, in love
Among open hearts,
By grace from above.

Dear Lord, I do not ask that Thou shouldst give me some
high work of Thine, some noble calling or some won-
drous task. Give me a little hand to hold in mine.

AUTHOR UNKNOWN

OPEN HOUSE, OPEN HEART

When John Todd was only six, both his parents died. A loving aunt sent her horse and a slave, Caesar, to get John. On the way home, John asked Caesar if his aunt would be there, if he would like living with her, if she would love him, if she would have things ready for him. Each time Caesar replied, "Oh, yes. You fall into good hands." When they arrived, his aunt was waiting with open arms and heart. She became his second mother, and he loved her dearly. Years later, as his aunt was nearing death, John wrote:

"My Dear Aunt, Years ago I left a house of death not knowing where I was to go, whether any-one cared, whether it was the end of me. The ride was long but . . . there we were in the yard and you embraced me and took me by the hand into my own room that you had made up. After all these years I still can't believe it—how you did all that for me! I was expected; I felt safe in that room—so welcomed. It was my room. Now it's your turn to go, and as one who has tried it out, I'm writing to let you know that Someone is waiting up. Your room is all ready, the light is on, the door is open, and as you ride into the yard—don't worry, Auntie. You're expected! I know. I once saw God standing in your doorway—long ago!"

> **YOU BUILT NO GREAT CATHEDRALS THAT CENTURIES APPLAUD, BUT WITH A GRACE EXQUISITE YOUR LIFE CATHEDRALED GOD.**
>
> THOMAS FESSENDEN

We are the temple of the living God. As God has said: "I will live with them and walk among them, and I will be their God, and they will be my people."

2 CORINTHIANS 6:16

A SPIRIT OF STRENGTH

The first memory that John H. Johnson has of his mother is of gripping her hand as they ran from the rampaging waters of a broken Mississippi River levee. The family lost everything, but "Miss Ger" was not one to quit. A field worker and later a domestic, she had known little but back-breaking work in her life. She had a dream, however, that her son would one day live in a city and become "somebody." She saved her money until she could move her family to Chicago. There, John graduated from high school with honors. When John had an idea for a magazine, it was his mother who came to his aid, allowing her new furniture to be used as collateral for a start-up loan. After *Negro Digest* became a success, John was able to do what he had dreamed about for years: he "retired" his mother, putting her on his personal payroll.

> MOTHERS ARE LIKE FINE COLLECTIBLES— AS THE YEARS GO BY THEY INCREASE IN VALUE.
>
> AUTHOR UNKNOWN

For fifty-nine years, John saw or talked to his mother almost every day. Even when he found himself in other nations, he called his mother daily—once, from atop a telephone pole in Haiti. He continued to draw upon her spiritual and physical toughness until she died. John went on to publish *Ebony* and *Jet* magazines, and his company owns three radio stations. He says, "Not a day passes that I don't feed off the bread of her spirit."

DESPISE NOT THY MOTHER WHEN SHE IS OLD.

PROVERBS 23:22 KJV

WISE WORDS

No force on earth can match
that of a mother's determination to fulfill a dream for her
child. She will sacrifice her
own needs and liberties, her
pleasures and her very life to
make a way for her own.
This is perhaps one of the
purest forms of altruism that
asks for no reward but to see
one's child step firmly,
securely, into a bright future.

ANNE SWEENEY

booklist

read more about it...listening

- *Listen with Your Heart*
  by Elizabeth Pantley
- *How to Talk So Kids Will Listen
  and Listen So Kids Will Talk*
  by Adele Faber, Elaine Mazlish

THE POWER OF HEARING

A YOUNG BOY CAME down to a pier on the mighty Mississippi River where an old man was fishing. He began to ask the man a myriad of questions, and with patience, the old man answered him. Their conversation was interrupted, however, by the shrill whistle of the River Queen as she came paddling downriver. Both the old man and boy stopped to stare in wonder as the gleaming ship splashed spray into the sunshine.

Above the noise of the paddle wheel, the boy began to call across the water, "Let me ride! Let me ride!" The old man tried to calm him, explaining that the River Queen didn't just stop anywhere and give rides to little boys. The boy cried all the louder, "Let me ride!" The old man stared in amazement as the great ship pulled toward shore and lowered a gangplank to the pier. In a flash the boy scampered onto the deck. As the gangplank was pulled aboard and the ship began to pull back into the mainstream, the boy called back to his newfound friend, "I knew this ship would stop for me, Mister. The captain is my father!"

The young boy was confident in his relationship with his father. As your children become confident that you will listen to them, they will be able to understand that their Heavenly Father will listen as well.

> **If we as** parents are too busy to listen to our children, how then can they understand a God who hears?
>
> V. GILBERT BEERS

Let the wise listen.

PROVERBS 1:5

Whatever is born of God OVERCOMES the world. And this is the victory that has overcome the world—our faith."

1 JOHN 5:4 NKJV

STEADFAST FAITH

As Louisa Stead, her husband, and their young daughter were enjoying an oceanside picnic one day, they noticed a young boy struggling in the surf. As the drowning boy cried out for help, Mr. Stead rushed to save him. Unfortunately, he was pulled under the waves by the terrified boy and both drowned as Louisa and her daughter watched helplessly from the shore.

In the sorrowful days that followed, the grief-stricken widow began to put pen to paper, and the result was a hymn known to millions:

'Tis so sweet to trust in Jesus, just to take Him at His word, just to rest upon His promise, just to know, "Thus saith the Lord."

O how sweet to trust in Jesus, just to trust His cleansing blood, just in simple faith to plunge me 'neath the healing, cleansing flood!

Yes, 'tis sweet to trust in Jesus, just from sin and self to cease, just from Jesus simply taking life and rest and joy and peace.

I'm so glad I learned to trust Thee, Precious Jesus, Savior, Friend; and I know that Thou art with me, wilt be with me to the end.

Trusting Jesus, Louisa went as a missionary to Africa, where she served the Lord for twenty-five years!

Who's Who:

Sarah

Sarah, the wife of Abraham, faced a life that didn't turn out as she had hoped. Even though God gave her and Abraham a promise that she would have a son, Sarah remained unable to conceive. As years passed, Sarah grew impatient and began to doubt God's promise. She took matters into her own hands, telling Abraham to take her maidservant, Hagar, as a wife and to try to build a family through her. Well, Hagar did become pregnant, and the family dynamics quickly became complicated. Dr. Phil would have had a remarkable "family in crisis" show with these two strong women and the apparently passive Abraham in the middle.

God still honored His promise and blessed Sarah with a son, bestowing the title "The Mother of Nations" on this presumably barren woman (Gen. 17:15). Sarah was amazed and grateful to God. She said in Genesis 21:6, "God has brought me laughter, and everyone who hears about this will laugh with me." Sarah's inability to wait for God, to trust fully in His promise, made life difficult and chaotic for her and for those around her. Yet God fulfilled His promise and blessed her.

A MOTHER'S HEART

Rachel had a close relationship with her mother, Maria, and after graduating from college, Rachel invited her mother to live with her. When Rachel's sister died, Rachel and Maria took in her two young daughters. Later, Rachel also took in her young nephew Roger and raised him as her own son. Maria kept house and typed Rachel's first two books, *Under the Sea-Wind* and *The Sea Around Us.*

> **Simply** having children does not make mothers.
>
> JOHN A. SHEDD

When her mother died in 1958, Rachel wrote: "Her love of life and of all living things was her outstanding quality. . . . And while gentle and compassionate, she could fight fiercely against anything she believed wrong, as in our present Crusade! Knowing how she felt about that will help me to return to it soon, and to carry it through to completion." Return, she did, writing *Silent Spring,* a book about the dangers of chemical pesticides—taking time out only to explore the woods with, read to, and play with Roger. The Environmental Protection Agency was formed in 1970, largely as a result of public outcry in the wake of her book.

Although she never married or bore children of her own, Rachel Carson is called by many, "mother of the age of ecology"—a genuine mother at heart.

Teach the young women to be sober . . . to love their children.

HENRY WARD BEECHER

✔ JUST DO IT

#1

Make a list of five children you know who need prayer. It may be your child's friend whose parents are splitting up, a child who's struggling with an illness or who's lost a parent—or perhaps it's a "high-risk" teen or even the boy who's bullied yours in school. Then pray this prayer for those children every day for one week:

Lord, I know these children are precious in Your sight. Please guide and comfort them, and put people in their paths who encourage them and point them to You. If I can be a part of that, please give me the grace and wisdom to know the right things to say and do. I thank You that You love and care about each one. Amen.

FAMILY *VACATION?*

> **PARENTHOOD: THAT STATE OF BEING BETTER CHAPERONED THAN YOU WERE BEFORE MARRIAGE.**
>
> MARCELENE COX

A COUPLE returned home after a week's vacation to the mountains feeling more exhausted than ever. All week they ran up and down mountain trails, valiantly struggling to keep their four children in line and safe from danger. Their tent had afforded them no privacy, and they were exhausted from playing referee around the campfire. The children, however, had had a great time. They bubbled over with enthusiasm as they told their grandparents about all the new sights, sounds, and experiences they had encountered— from roasting marshmallows to sleeping under the stars. The grandparents took one look at the parents, however, and said, "You need a vacation." The parents agreed, and, with the grandparents volunteering to babysit, they headed for a few days of rest at the beach.

After they had been there three days, they were sunning themselves one afternoon when the wife said dreamily, "Three whole days without the kids. That must be a record. I can't remember three whole days without the kids since the first one was born."

"Right," sighed her husband, and then added, "Believe it or not, I kind of miss them. Throw some sand in my face, will you?"

The joy of the Lord is your strength and stronghold.

NEHEMIAH 8:10 AMP

TOP **10** TIPS

That You Need a
Vacation from Your Kids

1. THE ONLY MUSIC YOU LISTEN TO IS PERFORMED BY DANCING PUPPETS.

2. YOU CAN'T RECALL YOUR LAST FULL NIGHT'S SLEEP.

3. YOUR PRAYERS START, END, AND CONSIST
WHOLLY OF THE WORDS, "FATHER, HELP PLEASE."

4. YOU HAVEN'T ENJOYED A HOT CUP OF COFFEE IN THREE YEARS.

5. YOUR ONLY ALONE TIME HAPPENS WHEN
YOUR HEAD HITS THE PILLOW EACH NIGHT.

6. YOU HAVEN'T BEEN ABLE TO FINISH A
MAGAZINE ARTICLE IN ONE SITTING.

7. AT 6:00 A.M. YOU START COUNTING
DOWN THE HOURS UNTIL BEDTIME.

8. YOU HAVEN'T EATEN A SINGLE MEAL
WHILE SEATED IN OVER A MONTH.

9. YOU SPEND MUCH OF THE DAY HIDING FROM YOUR CHILDREN.

10. RECENTLY, YOU'VE BEEN REFERRING TO
YOUR HUSBAND AS "WHAT'S HIS NAME . . .?"

PERSEVERING KINDNESS

A NUMBER OF YEARS AGO, a young girl known as "Little Annie" was locked in the dungeon of a mental institution outside Boston—the only place, said the doctors, for the hopelessly insane. At times, Annie behaved like an animal, attacking those who came close to her "cage." At other times, she sat in a daze.

An elderly nurse held hope for all God's children, and she began taking her lunch break in the dungeon, just outside Little Annie's cage. She hoped in some way to communicate love to her. One day she left her dessert—a brownie—next to Annie's cage. Annie made no response, but the next day, the nurse found the brownie had been eaten. Every Thursday thereafter, she brought a brownie to Annie.

As weeks passed, doctors noticed a change in Little Annie. After several months, they moved her upstairs. And eventually, the day came when this "hopeless case" was told she could return home. By that time, however, Annie was an adult, and she chose to stay at the institution to help others. One of those she cared for, taught, and nurtured was Helen Keller. Little Annie's full and proper name was Anne Sullivan.

Your children become the embodiment of the love you pour into them. Pour generously!

lighten up

A little girl was diligently pounding away on her mother's word processor. "What are you doing?" her mother asked. "I'm writing a story," she told her mother proudly. "Really," her mother wondered. "What's it about?" Without missing a keystroke, the little girl answered, "How should I know? I can't read!"

A doting mom wasn't sure if her son had learned his colors at preschool, so she decided to test him. Pointing at one thing after another, she would ask him what color it was. The little boy answered correctly each time, but finally he sighed and told his mother quite authoritatively, "Mom, I think you should try to figure out some of these yourself!"

Children are likely to live up to what

As he
thinketh
in his **heart,**
so is he.

PROVERBS 23:7 KJV

you believe of them. LADY BIRD JOHNSON

CONSIDER
THIS!

Do not provoke your children to anger, but bring them up in the discipline and instruction of the Lord.

EPHESIANS 6:4 NRSV

Children are much less impacted by the circumstances of your life together than by the response they see that you, the parent, have to them. It's these responses that imprint and then shape the way your children will react to situations in life. If you want to see children who show qualities such as mercy, humility, kindness, strength, and forbearance, children who can stand up under pressure, it is critical for them to see you exemplify the same.

Admit your failings to your kids. It doesn't show them that you're weak, but that there is strength in honesty and humility.

LITTLE WORDS, BIG IMPACT

In 1957 Ford bragged about producing "the car of the decade": the Edsel. One analyst likened its sales graph to a very dangerous ski slope. There is only one recorded case of an Edsel being stolen. These and many other such "failures" are listed in a book entitled *The Incomplete Book of Failures.* Appropriately, the book itself had two missing pages when it was printed! The book reports mistakes and errors in a variety of categories, including a memo from a record company that turned down the Beatles in 1962: "We don't like their sound. Groups of guitars are on their way out."

Maxie Baughan, a former all-pro linebacker, once came off the

NEVER, NEVER BE TOO PROUD TO SAY, "I'M SORRY" TO YOUR CHILD WHEN YOU'VE MADE A MISTAKE.

field and disgustedly threw his helmet to the ground. What he didn't know was that cameras had caught his display of bad temper. A few days later, he was watching his five-year-old son play, and suddenly the boy took off his helmet and gave it a heave. Baughan scolded him for poor sportsmanship, but then the boy told his dad about watching him do the same thing on TV.

Baughan promptly apologized.

Not apologizing for a mistake is to make two mistakes, and the second can be far more damaging!

Confess your faults one to another, and pray one for another.

JAMES 5:16 KJV

"You know children are GROWING UP when they start asking questions that have answers."

JOHN J. PLOMB

JUST THE FACTS, MA'AM

A little girl once asked her grandmother, "How old are you?" The grandmother replied, "Now dear, you shouldn't ask people that question. Most grown-ups don't like to tell their age."

The next day the little girl had another question. She asked, "Grandma, how much do you weigh?" The grandmother said, "Oh, honey, you shouldn't ask grown-ups how much they weigh. It isn't polite."

The third day the little girl came to her grandmother with a big smile and announced, "Grandma, I know how old you are. You're sixty-two. And I also know that you weigh 140 pounds."

"My goodness," the grandmother said, "how do you know all that?"

The little girl replied, "You left your driver's license on the table, and I read it." And then the little girl added, "And I also saw on your driver's license that you flunked sex."

Three of the greatest things a parent can ever do are:

1) answer a child's questions to the full extent the child is capable of understanding an answer, 2) give a child information they need to have and spare them knowledge they don't need, and 3) take time to converse with your child. Each is a genuine act of love!

Who's Who:

Abraham

In Genesis, chapter 22, we read about Abraham and his son, Isaac. Isaac was the literal fulfillment of his father's promise from God—flesh and blood evidence that God would keep His word to Abraham and make him the father of many nations.

It must have seemed ridiculous to Abraham that God would ask him to sacrifice his precious boy. And yet, Abraham was determined to obey God completely. They forged forward to the place where God had told him to carry out the sacrifice, trusting that God would not allow the unthinkable to happen.

As father and son approached the place where the sacrifice was to take place, Isaac asked, "The fire and wood are here, but where is the lamb for the burnt offering?" Abraham could have responded in a number of ways to his son's natural and innocent question. He could have told Isaac to go and search for a lamb, maybe buy a little time. He might have chosen the moment to actually explain God's request. Instead, Abraham said, "God himself will provide the lamb for the burnt offering, my son." That answer reveals the deep love and respect Abraham had for his only son. He took care to answer Isaac truthfully. His answer was satisfactory to Isaac, but it didn't give too much information for the time and circumstance.

God gave Abraham the ultimate test—and against every inclination a parent has for the preservation of his children, Abraham remained obedient to God. The Lord did not allow Abraham to harm Isaac and, as Abraham said, God himself provided the sacrifice—a ram.

HOW Do YOU MEASURE Up?

Having trouble finding the joy in motherhood? Are your children driving you nuts? Take this little quiz to get a read on your state of mind:

1. When I wake up in the morning, I:
   A. Greet the new day with verve and vigor.
   B. Pull the covers over my head and pretend I live alone.
   C. Feel as if I need a nap.
   D. Cry.

2. When my children awake in the morning, I:
   A. Greet them with a hug and a smile.
   B. Think, "Oh, no, not them again."
   C. Pretend I'm babysitting.
   D. Run.

3. Morning in my house feels like:
   A. A lively, happy place.
   B. A chaotic, but acceptable place.
   C. A crazy, stressful place.
   D. A clash between enemy tribes.

4. I spend my day feeling like:
   A. I can handle the unpredictability of parenting and still complete my "to do" list.
   B. I'll muddle through, somehow.
   C. I'm living for bedtime.
   D. I'd like to visit a correctional facility for a spell for some nice quiet time to myself.

5. After my children are in bed at night, I:
   A. Enjoy some downtime and reflect on my day.
   B. Say "Yahoo!" enthusiastically, but not too loudly.
   C. Fall into a heap on the couch amid three unfolded loads of laundry.
   D. Jump on their beds, scream out their names repeatedly, and say, "See, how do you like being awakened from a deep sleep?"

   If you answered "C" or "D" to every question, you may need to find time away without your children to gain some perspective. If you answered "A" to every question, you either should be leading parenting seminars or getting real. In truth, any mom could give any of the above answers in a given day, and, with the exception of waking one's own children, which no parent in her right mind would ever do, it's okay.

   Parenting is a mixed bag, one that requires help and resourcefulness. For every season of parenting, ask God to give you what you need to get through. And always remember the value of honesty and a big dose of humor.

THE LIGHTER SIDE

WOMEN SHOULD NOT HAVE CHILDREN AFTER 35— 35 CHILDREN ARE ENOUGH.

A mother already had five children under the age of ten when she gave birth to twins. The minister who came to see her in the hospital said, "I see the Lord has smiled on you again."

"Smiled?" the woman shrieked. "He laughed right out loud!"

Another woman once said to her visiting minister, "I thank God for my sons."

The minister replied, "I'm sure they're all good, productive citizens."

She replied, "Oh, yes. The firstborn is a doctor, the second became a lawyer, the third is a chemist, the fourth an artist, and the fifth a writer." The minister was obviously impressed, and then she added, "But thank God my husband and I had a dry goods store. Not a big one, mind you, but it's still enough for us to be able to support them all."

And finally there was the mother who remarked, "When I was young, my parents told me what to do. Now my children all tell me what to do. When is it that I get to do what I want to do?"

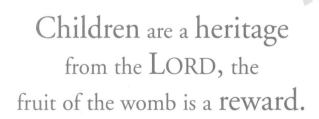

Children are a heritage
from the LORD, the
fruit of the womb is a reward.

PSALM 127:5 NKJV

THE SECRET OF CONTENTMENT

In *Little Women*, Mrs. March tells this story to her daughters, who unfortunately found they could "identify" with every word: "Once upon a time, there were four girls, who had enough to eat and drink and wear, a good many comforts and pleasures, kind friends and parents . . . and yet they were not contented. . . . These girls . . . made many excellent resolutions; but they . . . were constantly saying, 'If we only had this,' or 'If we could only do that.' So they asked an old woman what spell they could use to make them happy, and she said, 'When you feel discontented, think over your blessings, and be grateful.'

> **An infallible** way to make your child miserable is to satisfy all his demands.
>
> HENRY HOME

"They decided to try her advice, and soon were surprised to see how well off they were. One discovered that money couldn't keep shame and sorrow out of rich people's houses; another that . . . she was a great deal happier with her youth, health, and good spirits than a certain fretful, feeble old lady, who couldn't enjoy her comforts; a third that, disagreeable as it was to help get dinner, it was harder still to have to go begging for it; and the fourth, that even carnelian rings were not so valuable as good behavior. So they agreed to stop complaining, to enjoy the blessings already possessed."

Remember, not everything your child wants is best for them. The best way to bring happiness to your child is to teach them it comes from within.

Wise discipline imparts wisdom; spoiled adolescents embarrass their parents.

PROVERBS 29:15 MSG

✓ JUST DO IT

Set an example for your children by consciously developing the habit of thankfulness. Read this lovely prayer each night before you go to sleep and then praise God for your own list of blessings:

Accept, O Lord, our thanks and praise for all that You have done for us. We thank You for the splendor of the whole creation, for the beauty of this world, for the wonder of life, and for the mystery of love. We thank You for the blessing of family and friends and for the loving care that surrounds us on every side. We thank You for setting us at tasks which demand our best efforts, and for leading us to accomplishments which satisfy and delight us. We thank You also for those disappointments and failures that lead us to acknowledge our dependence on You alone. Above all, we thank You for Your Son Jesus Christ; for the truth of His Word and the example of His life; for His steadfast obedience, by which He overcame temptation; for His dying, through which He overcame death; and for His rising to life again, in which we are raised to the life of Your kingdom. Grant us the gift of Your Spirit, that we may know Him and make Him known; and through Him, at all times and in all places, may we give thanks to You in all things. *Amen.*

Book of Common Prayer

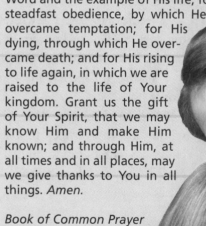

CONTINUING ED.

ADULT EDUCATION IS SOMETHING THAT WILL CONTINUE AS LONG AS KIDS HAVE HOMEWORK.

BILL COSBY HAS written in *Fatherhood* this humorous account about parents and homework:

When your child is struggling in school, you have such a strong desire to help that you often find it easier just to do the work yourself than to use a middleman. A few weeks ago my daughter came to me and said, "Dad, I'm in a bind. I've got to do this paper right away."

"All right," I said, "what's your plan of work?"

"You type it for me."

Once again, I typed her paper; but when I had finished and looked at the work, I said, "I'm afraid there's just one problem."

"What's that?" she said.

"This is awful. As your secretary, I can't let you turn this in."

Needless to say, I rewrote it for her, and I picked up a B minus. I would have had a B plus if I hadn't misspelled all those words.

And so, I've now done high school at least twice, probably closer to three times; and I've gone through college a couple of times too.

God will yet **fill** your mouth
with **laughter** . . . and your lips
with **joyful** shouting.

JOB 8:21 AMP

TOP **10** TIPS for Making Homework Less Stressful (for Everyone!)

1. EXPECT HOMEWORK, AND ACCEPT IT AS A PART OF YOUR FAMILY LIFE WHEN YOU HAVE SCHOOL-AGE CHILDREN.

2. ESTABLISH A STANDARD PLACE WHERE HOMEWORK IS DONE.

3. CREATE A BOX WHICH CONTAINS ALL THE BASICS THEY'LL NEED TO DO THEIR HOMEWORK.

4. COMMUNICATE ABOUT HOMEWORK ON A DAILY BASIS.

5. FIGURE OUT A REWARD SYSTEM THAT HELPS TO MOTIVATE THEM THROUGH THEIR ASSIGNMENTS.

6. TRY TO HELP YOUR CHILD THINK REALISTICALLY ABOUT HOW LONG THEIR ASSIGNMENTS WILL TAKE.

7. HELP YOUR CHILD TO THINK THROUGH THE DIRECTIONS OF AN ASSIGNMENT.

8. BE A RESOURCE, BUT NOT A RELEASE FROM RESPONSIBILITY.

9. MAKE SURE YOUR CHILD HAS SOME DOWNTIME IN THE DAY.

10. PRAY FOR YOUR CHILDREN, FOR CLARITY AND HELP. AND PRAY FOR STRENGTH AND PATIENCE FOR YOU.

SHARE AND SHARE ALIKE

THE MOTHER OF THREE small children, each born only two years apart, often found herself exhausted by the end of a day. Along with the children's father, she had set strict rules that after a story time, prayers, one small drink of water, and a final trip to the bathroom, each child must go to bed and stay there.

One night, after a particularly trying day, all three children were finally tucked into bed, and the parents headed to the kitchen for some cookies, milk, solitude, and a little time alone together. They had just started to relax when they suddenly found themselves surrounded by three little people, all standing in silence as they watched Mom and Dad each bite into a delicious home-baked cookie. Turning to Dad, Mom asked, "Well, do we relent, or do we stick with the rules?"

Before Dad could answer, their three-year-old daughter piped up, "Stick with the rules, Mom!"

Knowing that her daughter didn't really want to be sent back to bed, Mom asked, "And what exactly are those rules, dear?"

Her daughter replied without hesitation, "Share with one another."

lighten up

After putting her children to bed, a mom changed into old slacks and a droopy blouse and leaned over the sink to wash her hair. As she proceeded, she could hear her children becoming more and more rambunctious in the bedroom. Her patience was running thin.

At last, she wrapped a towel around her head and stormed into the dark bedroom. In her harshest voice, she ordered everyone back into bed and warned that there would be serious penalties for those who failed to quiet down and go to sleep. As she left the room, she heard her three-year-old say with a trembling voice, "Who was THAT?"

Discipline your children; you'll be glad you did—

"The persons **hardest** to convince they're at **retirement** age are **children** at **bedtime.**"

they'll turn out delightful to live with. PROVERBS 29:17 MSG

Trivia

Fun

Can you match these mothers from the Bible with their children?

1. Elizabeth (Luke 1:57-60)
2. Hannah (1 Samuel 2:18-21)
3. Jochebed (Exodus 6:20)
4. Ruth (Ruth 4:13-17)
5. Rachel (Genesis 30:22-24)
6. Eve (Genesis 4)
7. Rebekah (Genesis 25:20-24)
8. Eunice (2 Timothy 1:5; 3:14-15)
9. Sarah (Genesis 17:17-19)
10. Bathsheba (2 Samuel 12:24)

A. Samuel
B. Joseph
C. Obed
D. Cain and Able
E. John the Baptist
F. Jacob and Esau
G. Timothy
H. Aaron & Moses
I. King David
J. Isaac

1. John the Baptist; 2. Samuel; 3. Aaron and Moses; 4. the mother of Obed, the grandmother of Jesse, and the great-grandmother of David; 5. Joseph; 6. Cain and Abel; 7. Jacob and Esau; 8. Timothy, 9. Isaac; 10. King David

WALKING THE TALK

Don't **wander** off from
your **mother's teaching.**

PROVERBS 6:20 MSG

The story is told of four scholars who were arguing over the beauty and accuracy of various Bible translations.

One scholar argued for the *King James Version,* citing its beautiful, eloquent old English.

The second scholar advocated for the *American Standard Bible.* He cited its literalism, the way it moved a reader from passage to passage with confident feelings of accuracy from the original texts.

The third scholar said he preferred the translation by Moffatt. He praised its quaint, penetrating use of words, the turn of a phrase that captured the attention of the reader.

After giving thought to each of the lengthy and impassioned arguments presented, the fourth scholar said, "Frankly, I have always preferred my mother's translation."

Knowing that his mother was not a Bible translator, nor a scholar, the other three chuckled and said, "No, seriously. . . ." The man stood his ground. "I stand by my claim," he said. "My mother translated each page of the Bible into life. And it was the most convincing translation I have ever seen."

Dear Mother—You know that
nothing can ever change what
we have always been and
will always be to each other.

FRANKLIN ROOSEVELT

CONSIDER THIS!

How aware are you of what your kids pick up from you every day? As parents, it's safe to assume that the answer is: everything. The Bible says that believers in Christ should live in the Spirit. So often, people view life as what one does outside one's home—not behind closed doors when interacting with family. Yet this is where it's hardest and most important (and necessary) to seek to live by the light of God's Spirit. Being a parent brings you to the end of yourself and then asks for more.

If parents strive to live by the Spirit, and the fruits of the Spirit are evident in their lives, children will see this light. They'll be drawn to it, and they will want to emulate what they see in you. There's nothing greater than to have your children drawn to God because of what they see in your life.

The fruit of the Spirit is love, joy, peace, patience, kindness, goodness, faithfulness, gentleness and self-control. . . .
Since we live by the Spirit, let us keep in step with the Spirit.
GALATIANS 5:22-23,25

SHINING EXAMPLE

Benjamin Franklin came to a personal conclusion that the lighting of streets would not only add gentility to his city, but also make his city safer. In seeking to interest the people of his native Philadelphia in street lighting, however, he didn't try to persuade them by talking about street lighting. Instead, he hung a beautiful lantern on a long bracket before his own door. Then he kept the glass brightly polished and carefully and diligently lit the wick every evening just as dusk approached.

People wandering down the dark street saw Franklin's light a long way off. They found its glow not only friendly and beautiful, but a point of helpful guidance. Before long, other neighbors began placing lights on long brackets before their own homes. Soon, the entire city was dotted with such lights, and the entire city awoke to the value of street lighting. The matter was taken up with interest and enthusiasm as a citywide, city-sponsored endeavor.

Just as Franklin lit a lantern for his city, so, too, our actions as parents are like beacons to our children. What they see, they copy. And when what they see is good, what they copy is also good!

> IF YOU WANT YOUR CHILD TO ACCEPT YOUR VALUES WHEN HE REACHES HIS TEEN YEARS, THEN YOU MUST BE WORTHY OF HIS RESPECT DURING HIS YOUNGER DAYS.
>
> WILLIAM JAMES

We offer ourselves as a model for you,
so that you might follow our example.

2 THESSALONIANS 3:9 NASB

GOOD WORD FROM HOME

Her letters to her son Johannes give a strong impression of her clear common sense and her great kindheartedness. In these long letters, carefully preserved, she tells her son all the interesting news from Hamburg and never speaks ill of anybody. When son Fritz lost an excellent job, she wrote to Johannes: "Fritz must put his trust in God, who guides all human destinies. He will lead him out of this darkness." She remembered Johannes daily in her prayers, as well as Elise and Fritz, and tried to keep a tight bond among her children, reminding Johannes to remember their birthdays. There is no sign in her letters of any disharmony in her marriage, which lasted thirty-four years, and generally speaking, peace and cheerfulness seemed to prevail in her household.

WHEN MOTHER TERESA RECEIVED HER NOBEL PRIZE, SHE WAS ASKED, "WHAT CAN WE DO TO PROMOTE WORLD PEACE?" SHE REPLIED, "GO HOME AND LOVE YOUR FAMILY."

In sharp contrast was the world outside their home: a poverty-stricken slum with narrow, crooked streets and grime-encrusted, "blackened" frame houses. Disease was rampant, and if fire broke out, the effects in the neighborhood were devastating.

What was the impact of this mother's goodness and nurture on her son? There's no telling. Through the centuries, the compelling, beautiful music of Johannes Brahms has touched countless millions.

LET LOVE AND FAITHFULNESS NEVER LEAVE YOU;
BIND THEM AROUND YOUR NECK,
WRITE THEM ON THE TABLET OF YOUR HEART.

PROVERBS 3:3

WISE WORDS

I expect to pass through
this world but once; any
good thing therefore that
I can do, or any kindness
that I can show to any
fellow creature, let me do
it now; let me not defer or
neglect it, for I shall not
pass this way again.

AUTHOR UNKNOWN

SETTING THE RIGHT COURSE

NEAR THE TOP OF ONE OF the highest peaks in the Rocky Mountain range—more than 10,000 feet above sea level—are two natural springs. They are so close together and level in height that it would not take a great deal of effort to divert one streamlet toward the other. Yet if you follow the course of one of these streams, you will find that it travels easterly, and after traversing plateaus and valleys, receiving water from countless tributaries, it becomes part of the great Mississippi River and empties into the Gulf of Mexico.

If you follow the water from the other fountain, you will find that it descends gradually in a westerly direction, again combining with other tributaries until it becomes part of the Columbia River, which empties into the Pacific Ocean.

The terminal points of the two streams are more than five thousand miles apart, separated by one of the highest ranges of mountains in the world. And yet, at their onset, the two streams are close neighbors. Very little effort would be required to make the easterly stream run west, or the westerly stream run east.

If you want to impact the course of a life, start at birth!

> **Train your** child in the way in which you know you should have gone yourself.
>
> C.H. SPURGEON

[The Lord said,] "I will instruct you and teach you the way you should go; I will counsel you with my eye upon you."

PSALM 32:8 NRSV

new insights into ageless questions

I know I should be more confident about guiding my child toward a wise and Godly lifestyle, but somehow I often feel at a loss, especially in those areas that should be pretty simple and straight-forward—integrity, benevolence, discipline, for example. Where can I find a suitable source from which to draw good advice?

The book of Proverbs is an excellent, and often overlooked, parenting resource. It was written primarily by Solomon, one of the wisest men who ever lived, for the benefit of his own child. His succinct and powerful sayings are rich with advice for those who wish to live lives that are pleasing to God.

Reading one Proverb for each day of the month (there are 31 in all) is a great way to take in these wise words. Jot down the verses that seem fitting or helpful. The more you know about living God's way, the more you can pass along to your children. Try posting a few on the refrigerator for the benefit of your children. At the very least, they should begin a profitable dialogue.

CULTIVATING GEMS

> LET US **NOT** GROW **WEARY** IN DOING WHAT IS **RIGHT,** FOR WE WILL **REAP** AT HARVEST-TIME, IF WE DO **NOT GIVE UP.**
>
> GALATIANS 6:9 NRSV

AS A BOY IN Naples, he worked long hours in a factory, all the while yearning to be a singer. When he was ten years old, he took his first voice lesson. The teacher promptly concluded, "You can't sing. You haven't any voice at all. Your voice sounds like the wind in the shutters."

The boy's mother, however, heard greatness in her son's voice. She believed in his talent, and even though they were poor, she put her arms around him and said encouragingly, "My boy, I am going to make every sacrifice to pay for your voice lessons."

This mother's confidence in her son and her constant encouragement of him through the years paid off! Her boy became one of the most widely acclaimed singers around the world. His name? Enrico Caruso.

What is your child's special talent? His desire? What are your child's unique gifts—mentally, physically, spiritually? What more can you do to nurture them, even as you nurture your child?

Unearth and foster your child's gifts, and you truly have brought rare riches to the world.

A mother has, perhaps, the hardest earthly lot; and yet no mother worthy of the name ever gave herself thoroughly for her child who did not feel that, after all, she reaped what she had sown.

HENRY WARD BEECHER

TOP **10** TIPS

for Guiding
Your Child's Gifts

1. PRAY FOR WISDOM.

2. TAKE THE TIME TO RECOGNIZE YOUR CHILD'S STRENGTHS AND INCLINATIONS.

3. LOOK FOR HEALTHY AND AGE-APPROPRIATE WAYS FOR YOUR CHILD TO EXPRESS THEIR TALENTS.

4. ENCOURAGE YOUR CHILD WITH A LIGHT, BUT STEADY, HAND.

5. TAKE CARE TO DISTINGUISH YOUR DREAMS FROM YOUR CHILD'S.

6. BE CAREFUL NOT TO OVER-SCHEDULE YOUR CHILD.

7. DON'T BE AFRAID TO ALLOW OTHER ADULTS TO BRING OUT THE BEST IN YOUR CHILD.

8. FIGHT, AND SACRIFICE, IF NEED BE, TO MAKE A WAY FOR YOUR CHILDREN TO FULLY REALIZE AND EXPRESS THEIR GIFTS.

9. CONSISTENTLY PRAISE AND ENCOURAGE YOUR CHILDREN, BUT DON'T LET THEIR PERFORMANCE BECOME A MEASURE OF THEIR WORTH.

10. PROVIDE OPPORTUNITIES—AND THEN STAND BACK AND ENJOY!

booklist

read more about it...parenting

- *The Complete Book of Christian Parenting & Child Care: A Medical & Moral Guide to Raising Happy, Healthy Children*
  by William Sears, Martha Sears

- *Dare to Discipline*
  by Dr. James Dobson

- *Hints for Parents with Gospel Encouragements*
  by Gardiner Spring and Tedd Tripp

- *Parenting Today's Adolescent*
  by Bruce Nygren, Dennis and Barbara Rainey

SHAPING LITTLE LIVES

DR. ALBERT SIEGEL WAS quoted by the *Stanford Observer* as saying: "When it comes to rearing children, every society is only twenty years away from barbarism. Twenty years is all we have to accomplish the task of civilizing the infants who are born into our midst each year. These savages know nothing of our language, our culture, our religion, our values, our customs of interpersonal relations . . . communism, fascism, democracy, civil liberties, the rights of the minority, respect, decency, honesty, customs, conventions, and manners. The barbarian must be tamed if civilization is to survive."

A report from the Minnesota Crime Commission echoes this sentiment: "Every baby . . . wants what he wants when he wants it: his bottle, his mother's attention, his playmate's toy, his uncle's watch. Deny these and he seethes with rage and aggressiveness, which would be murderous were he not so helpless. This means that all children, not just certain children, are born delinquent. If permitted to continue in the self-centered world of infancy . . . every child would grow up a criminal."

The parent who does not punish wrongdoing by an infant permits it to be done by their teenager.

> **Train** up a child in the way he should go, even when he is old he will not depart from it.
> PROVERBS 22:6 NASB

A mother once asked a clergyman when she should begin the education of her child, . . . "Madam," was the reply, . . . "from the very first smile that gleams over an infant's cheek, your opportunity begins."

RICHARD WHATELY

"Of all the rights of women,
the GREATEST
is to be a mother."

LIN YUTANG

> Her children stand and bless her.
>
> Her husband praises her.
>
> PROVERBS 31:28 NLT

MOTHER MAKES THE MAN

After the famous food distributor Henry J. Heinz died, his will was found to contain this confession: "I desire to set forth at the very beginning of this will, as the most important item in it, a confession of my faith in Jesus Christ as my Savior. I also desire to bear witness to the fact that throughout my life, in which there were unusual joys and sorrows, I have been wonderfully sustained by my faith in God through Jesus Christ. This legacy was left me by my consecrated mother, a woman of strong faith, and to it I attribute any success I have attained."

Heinz is not the only famous American to credit his mother for his success, of course. Consider these words of another American hero, Thomas Edison: "I did not have my mother long, but she cast over me an influence which has lasted all my life. The good effects of her early training I can never lose. If it had not been for her appreciation and her faith in me at a critical time in my experience, I should never likely have become an inventor. I was always a careless boy, and with a mother of different mental caliber, I should have turned out badly. But her firmness, her sweetness, her goodness were potent powers to keep me on the right path. My mother was the making of me."

Although at times being a mother is the hardest job there is, it is also the greatest right.

Who's Who:

Hannah

Hannah wanted desperately to become a mother, but, for reasons we can't be certain of, the Lord "closed her womb" (1 Samuel 1). One day when Hannah was feeling particularly despondent about her situation, she went to the temple and poured out her heart to God. Hannah made a vow: if God would give her a son, she would give the child to the Lord. God answered her prayer, and Hannah gave birth to Samuel.

Hannah brought Samuel to live at the temple at a very young age. Surely she experienced grief at leaving her son, but she also rejoiced at the privilege of being a mother—the mother of Samuel, who was to become a great prophet of the Lord. When she brought Samuel to the temple, she prayed: "My heart rejoices in the LORD; in the LORD my horn is lifted high. My mouth boasts over my enemies, for I delight in your deliverance" (Samuel 2:1).

Hannah knew the joy of longing fulfilled and the understanding of the privilege and responsibility of having a child. God blessed Hannah with three more sons and two daughters. While Hannah did not have the opportunity to raise Samuel, she did see him grow into a great man of God.

NO TIME FOR WORRY

A BUSINESSMAN ONCE made a "Worry Chart" on which he kept a record of all his worries. After a year, he tabulated the results. He found that 40 percent of the things he had worried about were now things that were very unlikely to happen; 30 percent were worries about past decisions he had made and which he could not now unmake; 12 percent dealt with other people's criticism of him; and 10 percent were worries about his future health, only about half of which he could do anything about in the present. In all, he concluded that only about 8 percent of his worries over the previous year had been legitimate.

What is it that you are worried about today? Most days? Keeping a worry chart might be a good way of discovering what it is that truly concerns you most.

Of equal interest in weighing one's worries would be a "Prayer Chart." What is it that you pray about the most? When asked to tabulate their prayers, many people seem to find that they actually spend very little time praying about the things that concern them the most!

Convert your worry time into prayer time.

It's not only a more productive activity, but a healthier and more enjoyable one.

lighten up

A mom tells a story about saying bedtime prayers with her little girl. First the little girl listed all the things she was thankful for—including ketchup. Then she listed all the things she wanted God to do—including making her brother be nice to her. Finally, as an afterthought, she added, "Oh yeah, God, if there's anything I can do for You, just let me know."

Do not be anxious about anything, but in everything, by prayer And the peace of God, which transcends all understanding, will

66 A problem not worth praying about
isn't worth worrying about. 99

and petition, with thanksgiving, present your requests to God.
guard your hearts and your minds in Christ Jesus. PHILIPPIANS 4:6-7

CONSIDER
THIS!

The word "discipline" is used 20 times in the book of Proverbs, five times giving specific commands to parents about correcting their children. Proverbs 19:18 says, "Discipline your son, for in that there is hope." Scripture also teaches that God disciplines His children. Psalm 94:12 says, "Blessed is the man You discipline, O LORD." God's children are fortunate when He disciplines because this is an expression of love—God cares enough to want to bring about the best in those who follow Him.

Good, consistent discipline won't warp your children or stifle their creativity. On the contrary, kids feel the ease to be creative and live fully within the loving boundaries you place on them.

HOLDING THE LINE

In *Dare to Discipline,* Dr. James Dobson tells about his own mother's approach: "I found her reasonable on most issues. If I was late coming home from school, I could just explain what had caused the delay. . . . If I didn't get my work done, we could sit down and come to some kind of agreement for future action. But there was one matter on which she was absolutely rigid: She did not tolerate 'sassiness.'

"She knew that backtalk and 'lip' are the child's most potent weapons of defiance and they must be discouraged." Through the years, Dobson recalls having been spanked with a shoe, and often with a handy belt. He vividly recalls, however, one particular spanking. He made the costly mistake of sassing his mother when the only object nearby for a spanking was her girdle. He says, "Now those were the days when a girdle was a weapon. It weighed about sixteen pounds and was lined with lead and steel . . . with a multitude of straps and buckles. . . . She gave me an entire thrashing with one massive blow!"

While Jim may not have appreciated her principles about discipline at the time, he certainly did in later years. His book *The Strong-Willed Child* is dedicated to her!

> **THE BEST ACADEMY IS A MOTHER'S KNEE.**
>
> JAMES RUSSELL LOWELL

Discipline your son,
and he will give you peace; he will
bring delight to your soul.

PROVERBS 29:17

A LEGACY OF POTENTIAL

Samuel Blackwell was an intelligent and warm-hearted man, an enthusiastic supporter of religious tolerance, women's rights, and the abolition of slavery. When his children were barred from public schools because of his religious convictions, he hired private tutors for them. As a result, they received an even better education than they would have had—the girls pursuing the same course of study as the boys. His wife, Hannah, encouraged a love of music and reading in her children. Their home was a magnet for intellectuals of the period, and from their earliest years, the children were exposed to people who valued clear thinking, social awareness, and new ideas. Above all, the Blackwell children were accepted as equals by their parents and given major doses of loving approval.

> IF A CHILD LIVES WITH APPROVAL, HE LEARNS TO LIVE WITH HIMSELF.
>
> DOROTHY LAW NOLTE

Five Blackwell girls had careers: Elizabeth and Emily as doctors, Anna a newspaper correspondent, Marian a teacher, Ellen an author and artist. One of their sons, Samuel, married America's first woman minister, Antoinette Brown. Son Henry married Lucy Stone, the women's rights leader. All this in an age when women were not allowed to serve on juries, cast ballots, testify in courts, and were barred from most higher education and from many professions!

When a parent shows his or her approval of children and their talents, the children never learn to limit their abilities.

THEREFORE, ACCEPT ONE ANOTHER, JUST AS CHRIST ALSO ACCEPTED US TO THE GLORY OF GOD.

ROMANS 15:7 NASB

WISE WORDS

Education is simply the soul of a society as it passes from one generation to another.

G.K. CHESTERTON

You shall put these words of mine in your heart and soul, and you shall bind them as a sign on your hand, and fix them as an emblem on your forehead. Teach them to your children, talking about them when you are at home and when you are away, when you lie down and when you rise. Write them on the doorposts of your house and on your gates, so that your days and the days of your children may be multiplied in the land.

DEUTERONOMY 11:18-21 NRSV

A STICKY AFFAIR

A MOTHER FINDS OUT WHAT IS MEANT BY SPITTING IMAGE WHEN SHE TRIES TO FEED CEREAL TO HER BABY.

IMOGENE FEY

IN *THE CHRISTIAN Mother,* Jacky Hertz writes: "However sweet and lovable, babies are still very inconsiderate and often dirty creatures. Will I ever forget one day as we were living in Sitka, Alaska? All I had to do while Bill worked eight hours a day on a new naval base nearby was to keep up the tiny two-room house and care for our first baby, then eleven months old. Surely, some would say, I could have cleaned the entire twenty-by-twenty-foot house in two hours a day and had leisure to spare. But life doesn't give us what we'd like.

"One day the baby had been quiet too long. I went to the bedroom to see if all that silence was really sleep. . . . The view that met my eyes made me want to turn and run crying, or beat my head against the wall. . . . But I only began to laugh, and then to dissolve in hysterical giggles. Being fairly new to motherhood, I'd carelessly pinned his diaper with only two pins, one on either side. Now I saw he had soiled the diaper and, being wide awake, had begun to play. . . . He'd smeared the sheet . . . the mattress . . . the bars of the crib . . . the bottoms of his feet . . . between his toes . . . his hands . . . his clothes . . . his face . . . his hair. Yet from the middle of all this unholy mess his eyes were so innocent!"

There is a **right** time for everything: . . . A time to **laugh.**

ECCLESIASTES 3:1,4 TLB

TOP **10** TIPS
for Surviving Life with Tots

1. HAVE STASHES OF WET WIPES EVERYWHERE.

2. BUY FAVORITE SNACKS IN BULK AND PORTION THEM OUT AHEAD OF TIME.

3. STICK TO A ROUTINE. IT WILL HELP YOUR CHILD FEEL SECURE AND KEEP YOU ORGANIZED.

4. BUY MULTIPLES OF THE NECESSITIES SO THAT YOU DON'T SPEND HALF OF YOUR TIME TRYING TO LOCATE THEM AND THE OTHER HALF TRYING TO CALM YOUR DEMANDING CHILD!

5. LIMIT THE NUMBER OF TOYS YOU HAVE OUT. IT HELPS WITH CLEANUP AND KEEPS THE KIDS FROM GETTING BORED AS YOU SWITCH OUT TOYS FROM TIME TO TIME.

6. SET STRICT BOUNDARIES AS TO WHERE KIDS CAN EAT IN YOUR HOUSE.

7. CHECK YOUR EXPECTATIONS—THERE'S ONLY SO MUCH YOU CAN DO WHEN YOU HAVE LITTLE ONES.

8. RECOGNIZE THE FUNNY SIDE—EVERYONE WILL BE HAPPIER FOR IT.

9. EVERY MORNING, ASK GOD TO GIVE YOU THE STRENGTH, HUMOR, AND PATIENCE YOU NEED.

10. REMEMBER THIS IS ONLY A SEASON, ONE THAT YOU WILL REMEMBER WITH FONDNESS (EVEN LONGING) WHEN YOUR CHILDREN ARE GROWN!

booklist

HAZARDS OF DRIVING

IN HIS BESTSELLER, *Fatherhood,* Bill Cosby tells of a decision that he and his wife made about their children using the family car: "We would not allow any of the children to have a driver's license as long as he or she was living with us." He asks, "Does this sound unreasonable to you?" Cosby goes on to write:

One memorable day, one of these children did drive to town just to see if she could do it while unencumbered by a license. It was a Saturday morning, and my wife and I had just finished breakfast. I walked over to the sink to rinse out a glass, and there I suddenly saw our car going past the kitchen window. Turning to my wife, I said, "Dear, did you just drive by here?"

"No," she replied.

"Well, am I in this kitchen?"

"As far as I can tell."

"Then why did I just go by in the car?"

> The **best way to** keep children at home is to make home a pleasant atmosphere—and to let the air out of the tires.
>
> DOROTHY PARKER

Encourage the young men to be self-controlled. In everything set them an example by doing what is good. In your teaching show integrity, seriousness and soundness of speech.

TITUS 2:6-8

MIND OF A CHILD

For all the "trouble" children can cause, they can also keep life fun with their unrehearsed quips and candid observations about life. Consider, for example, the little boy who was in a quandary about what to get his mother for Mother's Day. The little girl next door asked, "You have any money?"

"Na-a-a," the boy said. "What about making her something?" the girl asked. "I'm not very good at arts and crafts," the boy admitted.

> **"Let the little children** come to me . . . for the kingdom of God belongs to such as these."
>
> LUKE 18:16

"I know!" the little girl said. "You could promise to keep your room clean and neat for a whole week. And if you really want to make it a special gift, you could remember to clean your goldfish bowl and put your dirty clothes in the laundry basket."

The little boy just shrugged, unimpressed by her ideas. "Or," she continued doggedly, "you could go home the first time she calls you. Or . . . you could quit fighting with your brothers and sisters, especially at the dinner table."

The boy continued to shake his head. "No," he said. "I want to get my mom something she will really use—and something she'll really appreciate!"

A lot of **parents** pack up their **troubles** and **send** them off to summer **camp.**

JUST DO IT

#1

For those times when you need to remind yourself that your child is indeed made in the image and likeness of God, try this: Make a list of three unique attributes or strengths your child possesses (even if they aren't yet in their sanctified form).

#2

Focusing on these attributes, pray that God will develop and use these qualities in your child to bring about good in your home, in the world, and in His kingdom. Pray also that God will give you "eyes to see" the good in your children and give you the wisdom and strength to help them develop those gifts through all the phases, stages, and conflicts that are inevitable aspects of parenting.

#3

#4

#5

#6

#7

#8

#9

#10

"It is more blessed to GIVE than to receive."

ACTS 20:35 KJV

A MOTHER'S SACRIFICE

In 1932, Violet married a union organizer and within a few years had four sons. When she was pregnant a fifth time, gangsters moved to take over the union, and her husband left, feeling his family was safer without him. Violet and her sons moved into a tiny apartment, and a few months later, a daughter was born. To feed her family, Violet worked days at the National Silver Company and nights at a drugstore. She would work, have bouillon for lunch, finish her first job, pick up a kidney for twenty-five cents and make soup, tell the children not to mind the taste, go to the second job, come home and wash out the children's socks and shirts, catch a couple of hours of sleep, and begin her next day. On days off, she waited tables, and holidays, she worked at a department store.

Over the years she worked in a cracker factory, hawked ice cream, labeled medicine bottles, cleaned offices, and pushed a coffee cart. In 1959 she became an orderly in a home for the aged, and seventeen years later she retired with a pension of $31.78 a month. For the first time since 1946 she had a week off! Thomas, her son, perhaps paid her the highest tribute possible, saying he had only "happy memories" of his childhood: "We didn't even know we were poor until years later."

Who's Who:

Widow of Zarephath

The Widow of Zarephath—the Bible doesn't tell us her name, only that her husband died, leaving her alone to care for herself and their son in a foreign land. She must have considered breaking down many times, giving up, surrendering to the poverty, famine, and loss that overwhelmed her life. But she did not!

She held on and even befriended a stranger. When he asked for water, she complied. When he asked for a piece of bread, she apologized, telling him that she had only enough for one last meal for herself and her young son. When the man told her that he was a prophet of God, she must have been puzzled. Why would this man attempt to speak for God? She had no idea that the man was Elijah, a prophet on the run from King Ahab.

Still, something in his words made her willing to take a chance. "The jar of flour will not be used up and the jug of oil will not run dry until the day the LORD gives rain on the land" (1 Kings 17:14 NRSV). The widow of Zarephath did what the prophet told her, and she and her son were saved. She was willing to place her faith in a stranger and give what little she had left in order to save her child, and God honored her faith and sacrifice.

Read all about the Widow of Zarephath in 1 Kings 17:8-24.

EVERYTHING COUNTS

A poem first published in *The Bible Friend* speaks about the great influence that a mother has:

> I took a piece of plastic clay
> And idly fashioned it one day;
> And as my fingers pressed it still,
> It moved and yielded at my will.
> I came again when days were past,
> The form I gave it still it bore,
> And as my fingers pressed it still,
> I could change that form no more.
> I took a piece of living clay,
> And gently formed it day by day,
> And molded with my power and art,
> A young child's soft and yielding heart.
> I came again when days were gone;
> It was a man I looked upon,
> He still that early impress bore,
> And I could change it never more.

> **A torn** jacket is soon mended; but hard words bruise the heart of a child.
>
> HENRY WADSWORTH LONGFELLOW

Every word, every action, leaves a mark upon your child, for good or for bad. Little things to an adult sometimes loom large for a child. What may seem to you an insignificant comment or deed may turn out to be the one thing your child remembers!

I am writing these things . . . in accordance with the and not for tearing down.

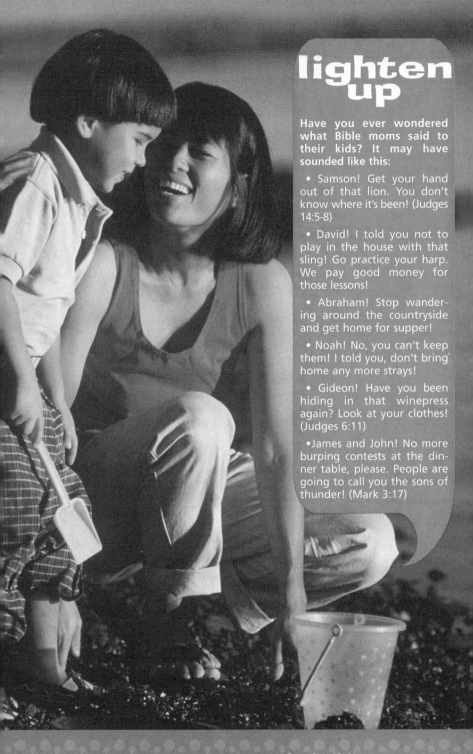

lighten up

Have you ever wondered what Bible moms said to their kids? It may have sounded like this:

• Samson! Get your hand out of that lion. You don't know where it's been! (Judges 14:5-8)

• David! I told you not to play in the house with that sling! Go practice your harp. We pay good money for those lessons!

• Abraham! Stop wandering around the countryside and get home for supper!

• Noah! No, you can't keep them! I told you, don't bring home any more strays!

• Gideon! Have you been hiding in that winepress again? Look at your clothes! (Judges 6:11)

•James and John! No more burping contests at the dinner table, please. People are going to call you the sons of thunder! (Mark 3:17)

authority which the Lord gave me for building up
2 CORINTHIANS 13:10 NASB

CONSIDER
THIS!

Meditate on this verbal picture of love from
1 Corinthians 13:4-8 MSG:

Love never gives up.
Love cares more for others than for self.
Love doesn't want what it doesn't have.
Love doesn't strut.
Love doesn't have a swelled head.
Love doesn't force itself on others.
Love isn't always "me first."
Love doesn't fly off the handle.
Love doesn't keep score of the sins of others.
Love doesn't revel when others grovel.
Love takes pleasure in the flowering of truth.
Love puts up with anything.
Love trusts God always.
Love always looks for the best.
Love never looks back.
Love keeps going to the end.

GIFT OF LOVE

One evening just before Mary Martin, the great Broadway musical star, was to go on stage in *South Pacific*, a note was handed to her. It was from Oscar Hammerstein, who had written this to her from his deathbed:

YOU MAY GIVE WITHOUT LOVING, BUT YOU CANNOT LOVE WITHOUT GIVING.

"Dear Mary, a bell's not a bell till you ring it. A song's not a song till you sing it. Love in your heart is not put there to stay. Love isn't love till you give it away."

After her performance that night a number of people rushed backstage, exclaiming, "Mary, what happened to you out there tonight? We have never heard anything like that performance! You sang with more power than you've ever sung!"

Blinking back tears, Mary then read them the note from Hammerstein and added, "Tonight, I gave my love away!"

Even the poorest person has something to give to others if he has love in his heart. Love's gifts take many forms—a smile, a hug, a note of thanks, "just being there" in tough times. Love is the one gift that always fits, is always appropriate, and is always in season and in fashion.

God so loved the world, that he gave his only begotten Son, that whosoever believeth in him should not perish, but have everlasting life.

JOHN 3:16 KJV

WORDS OF LIFE

> WE SHOULD **SEIZE** EVERY **OPPORTUNITY** TO GIVE ENCOURAGEMENT. **ENCOURAGEMENT** IS **OXYGEN** TO THE SOUL.
>
> GEORGE M. ADAMS

CHILDREN'S stories often provide profound insights into life. The tales of Winnie the Pooh are a good source for friendly and warm words, as evidenced by the following story told on a Pooh Bear recording:

One day Pooh Bear is about to go for a walk in the Hundred Acre wood. It's about 11:30 in the morning. It is a fine time to go calling—just before lunch. So Pooh sets out across the stream, stepping on the stones, and when he gets right in the middle of the stream he sits down on a warm stone and thinks about just where would be the best place of all to make a call.

He says to himself, "I think I'll go see Tigger." No, he dismisses that. Then he says, "Owl!" Then, "No, Owl uses big words, hard-to-understand words."

At last he brightens up! "I know! I think I'll go see Rabbit. I like Rabbit. Rabbit uses encouraging words like, 'How's about lunch?' and 'Help yourself, Pooh!' Yes, I think I'll go see Rabbit."

Give some oxygen—in the form of encouragement—to your child daily.

To make an apt answer is a joy to anyone, and a word in season, how good it is!

PROVERBS 15:23 NRSV

TOP **10** TIPS for Giving Encouragement to Your Children

1. MAKE TIME TO HAVE REAL CONVERSATIONS WITH YOUR CHILDREN.

2. NOTICE WHAT YOUR CHILDREN ARE DOING.

3. GIVE STICKERS OR TREATS AS REWARDS FOR ACCOMPLISHMENTS.

4. PRAY WITH YOUR CHILDREN. LET THEM HEAR YOU TELL GOD HOW THANKFUL YOU ARE FOR THEM.

5. IF YOU'VE DISCIPLINED YOUR CHILD, BE SURE TO TAKE TIME TO EXPRESS YOUR LOVE TO HIM AS WELL.

6. SET UP SITUATIONS WHERE YOUR CHILD CAN SUCCEED.

7. WRITE AN UNEXPECTED NOTE OR DROP A CARD IN THE MAIL FOR YOUR CHILD.

8. USE POSITIVE, ENCOURAGING LANGUAGE IN YOUR HOME AMONG EVERYONE IN THE FAMILY.

9. POST SCRIPTURES THAT REMIND EVERYONE TO SPEAK IN LOVE AND KINDNESS (EPHESIANS 4:32 OR 1 CORINTHIANS 13).

10. REMEMBER, "PLEASANT WORDS ARE A HONEYCOMB, SWEET TO THE SOUL AND LIKE HEALTH TO THE BODY" (PROVERBS 16:24 NRSV).

PAYING IT FORWARD

A reporter once interviewed the famous contralto Marion Anderson and asked her to name the greatest moment in her life. The reporter knew she had many big moments to choose from. He expected her to name the private concert she gave at the White House for the Roosevelts and the King and Queen of England. He thought she might name the night she received the $10,000 Bok Award as the person who had done the most for her hometown, Philadelphia. Instead, Marion Anderson shocked him by responding quickly, "The greatest moment in my life was the day I went home and told my mother she wouldn't have to take in washing anymore."

> LOVING A CHILD IS A CIRCULAR BUSINESS. . . . THE MORE YOU GIVE, THE MORE YOU GET, THE MORE YOU GET, THE MORE YOU GIVE.
>
> PENELOPE LEACH

The circular pattern of love between a parent and child is more than a matter of "what goes around, comes around." Rather, it stems from the principle that what a child sees, a child copies. Children are not born to be selfless and generous. Their more common cries are rooted in "Me first! Mine! I want." A child must learn to share, to sacrifice for others, to give spontaneously and from the heart. And a child learns that lesson quickly and most easily by copying someone else—usually their mother!

GIVE, AND IT WILL BE GIVEN TO YOU. . . .
FOR BY YOUR STANDARD OF MEASURE IT WILL BE
MEASURED TO YOU IN RETURN.

LUKE 6:38 NASB

WISE WORDS

Honor your father and your mother, as the LORD your God has commanded you, so that you may live long and that it may go well with you in the land the LORD your God is giving you.

DEUTERONOMY 5:16

booklist

- *Parenting with Scripture: A Topical Guide for Teachable Moments*
  by Kara Durbin

- *What the Bible Says About Parenting*
  by John MacArthur, Jr.

- *God's Great News for Children: Leading Your Child to Christ*
  by Rick Osborne, Marnie Wooding

- *I Believe in Jesus: Leading Your Child to Christ*
  by John MacArthur

LEGACY OF BELIEF

TWO BOYS WERE WALKING home from church one day. They began talking about the Sunday school lesson they had heard earlier in the morning.

"That would really be something," one of the boys said, "to be out in a wilderness for forty days and nights."

"Yeah," said the other boy, "and not eat. Jesus must have been real strong."

"It would have been kind of scary, too," said the first boy, "to have the devil show up and tempt you."

The second little boy didn't respond, so the first boy asked, "Do you believe that stuff about the devil? Do you think there really is a devil?"

The second little boy looked at his friend and said, "Naaah, he's probably just like Santa Claus—it's really just your dad."

Not only do children copy the mannerisms of their parents, they are quick to zero in on their parents' traits, beliefs, and values. Would your child call you a Christian today? Does your child know what you believe, and why? Does your child know how important your faith is to you?

The most important person to whom you can witness about your faith is your own child.

> **Let us** hold fast the profession of our faith without wavering.
>
> HEBREWS 10:23 KJV

Children miss nothing in sizing up their parents. If you are only half convinced of your beliefs, they will quickly discern that fact.

JAMES DOBSON

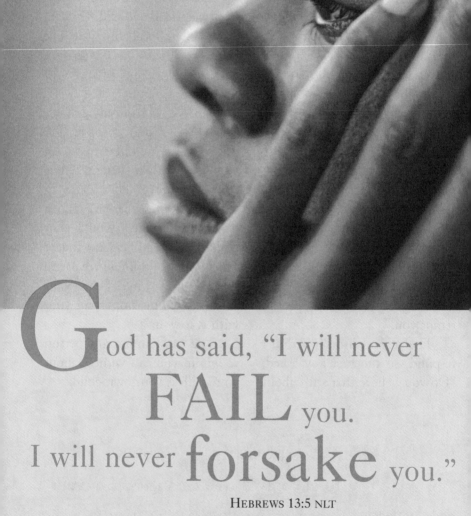

God has said, "I will never FAIL you. I will never forsake you."

HEBREWS 13:5 NLT

CARING THAT COUNTS

Leslie was born mentally retarded, without eyes, and with cerebral palsy. He was totally unresponsive to sound or touch. At the age of six months, he was expected to die shortly. A nurse, May Lemke, was asked if she could care for him at home until that time. She did—for more than thirty years.

When May accepted baby Leslie, she accepted him as just that, a baby—no different from others—to be taught and loved. Year after year she cared for him, but there was no movement or response. Even so, she never stopped talking to him, singing to him, or praying for him. Music filled their home—still, no response. She and her husband bought an old used piano and put it in his bedroom. She pushed his fingers against the keys. With quiet faith, she knew God would someday help Leslie to break out of his prison. She rejoiced when he began to walk at age 16.

Several years later, May and her husband were awakened one night by the sound of Tchaikovsky's Piano Concerto No. 1. Startled, they arose to find Leslie at the piano with a smiling glow on his face. Shortly thereafter he began to talk and to cry—and to sing. And at age 28, he began to talk in earnest. May's prayers were answered—in God's timing, God's way.

Who's Who:

Moses

Moses was born at a difficult time for Hebrew boys. The Jewish people were in captivity and serving as slaves to the Egyptian Pharaoh, and this hard-hearted ruler instructed that any Israeli baby boy should be tossed into the Nile River. Moses' mother protected him for as long as she could, but it soon became clear that she would need another plan.

Probably at the time, her only thought for her new baby was survival. It's not clear what circumstances or thinking prompted her to put her three-month-old baby into a basket and leave him at the river's edge, but she must have believed it was his best chance for staying alive. Of course, as the story goes in the book of Exodus, it was. The Hebrew baby captured the attention and heart of the Pharaoh's daughter, who found him and raised him as her own son.

Neither his mother nor his adoptive mother could have predicted that God would use this unlikely boy to lead the nation of Israel out of captivity. A mother's love and instinct to protect her child was the first important step in God's plan to release the Hebrew people from captivity and lead them into the Promised Land.

NEVER TOO EARLY

THE IMPORTANCE OF THE first few years of a child's life cannot be overestimated. It is during those years that the foundation is laid for a child's language ability, ethics, morality, and value systems. In his book, *All Men Are Brothers,* Mahatma Gandhi said this about the instilling of values in very early childhood: "I am convinced that for the proper upbringing of children the parents ought to have a general knowledge of the care and nursing of babies. . . . We labour under a sort of superstition that the child has nothing to learn during the first five years of its life. On the contrary, the fact is that the child never learns in later life what it does in its first five years. The education of the child begins with conception."

The famous psychoanalyst Sigmund Freud agreed. A Viennese woman once asked him, "How early should I begin the education of my child?"

Freud replied with a question of his own, "When will your child be born?"

"Born?" the woman asked. "Why, he is already five years old!"

"My goodness, woman," Freud cried, "don't stand there talking to me—hurry home! You have already wasted the five best years!"

> **The cure** of crime is not in the electric chair, but in the high chair.
>
> ELBERT HUBBARD

Train children in the right way, and when old, they will not stray.

PROVERBS 22:6 NRSV

new insights into ageless questions

Simply taking care of the physical needs of a baby, particularly an infant, is an all-consuming affair. Are there any simple,
proven ways to stimulate my child's mind and development in
the first five years of life and beyond?

Much of early education comes in the midst of everyday life. Here are a
few simple ways to begin teaching and awakening the sensibilities of
your little one as you go about your day:

- *Talk to your child* when you're changing, feeding, resting, folding laundry or driving.

- *Play classical music.* Classical music has been proven effective in stimu-
lating cognitive development, particularly in the areas of math and
organizational thinking.

- *Read, read, read to your baby,* your toddler, your four-year-old. Nothing
is as effective for language development as settling into a book with
your child. Include Bible stories, and introduce them to the themes
and characters of the Bible.

- *Use everyday events to teach your little ones* concepts like order of events,
opposite concepts ("in" and "out," "up" and "down," etc.).

- *Use baby signs* to stimulate cognitive development and to give your
baby tools to communicate prior to his or her talking.

- *Introduce prayer and Bible songs* into your repertoire. It's never to early
to start instilling knowledge of and a love for God and His Word.

HOW Do YOU MEASURE Up?

When it comes to giving your two cents, do you give a dollar? Take this little quiz to see if you put your money where your mouth is:

1. When I'm in a discussion with a group of people, do I feel that I:
   A) Must contribute, regardless of my knowledge of a subject?
   B) Monopolize the conversation, so I can have the floor?
   C) Can sit back, listen, and speak if I'm sure I have something worth contributing?

2. When talking with close friends or family, do I:
   A) Constantly think of the next thing I'm going to say and jump in at the first pause?
   B) Monopolize the conversation, because I am, after all, the brightest bulb on my family tree?
   C) Really listen to what others are saying and then form my response?

3. When my children talk to me, do I:
   A) Pretend that I'm listening and give appeasing "um hmms" as I continue moving around the house?
   B) Interrupt and talk over them?
   C) Take the time (when truly possible) to look them in the eyes, listen, and then respond?

The above little quiz is exaggerated (although everyone knows someone who can't seem to stop talking), but it is a means of evaluating where you fall between monopolizing conversation and tuning in to what people are saying. As it says in James 1, it is wise to be quick to listen and slow to speak in all circumstances.

GOLDEN SILENCE

> I REGRET
> OFTEN THAT I
> HAVE SPOKEN;
> NEVER THAT
> I HAVE
> BEEN SILENT.
>
> SYRUS

During World War I, Eleanor Roosevelt made a valiant effort to conserve food, but things didn't turn out exactly as she had planned. In July 1917 the Food Administration picked their household as "a model for other large households." *The New York Times* sent a newswoman to interview Mrs. Roosevelt about her food-saving methods, and she later wrote: "Mrs. Roosevelt does the shopping, the cooks see that there is no food wasted, the laundress is sparing in her use of soap, each servant has a watchful eye . . . and all are encouraged to make helpful suggestions in the use of 'left-overs.'" The article ended with a quote from Mrs. Roosevelt: "Making ten servants help me do my saving has not only been possible but also highly profitable."

As might be expected, the story created a great deal of mirth in Washington. FDR joined in teasing his wife, saying, "Please have a photo taken showing the family, the ten cooperating servants, the scraps saved from the table, and the handbook." To which Mrs. Roosevelt moaned in reply, "I feel dreadfully about it because so much is not true and yet some of it I did say. I will never be caught again, that's sure, and I'd like to crawl away for shame."

When in doubt about what to say, say nothing.

When words are many, sin is not absent,
but he who holds his tongue is wise.

PROVERBS 10:19

WHO'S THE BOSS?

A PERFECT EXAMPLE OF MINORITY RULE IS A BABY IN THE HOUSE.

MILWAUKEE JOURNAL

JEAN KERR shares these secrets about feeding an infant in *How I Got to Be Perfect:* "Some adults who find themselves uneasy in the silence have discovered that it is helpful to intone, rhythmically, the names of the entire family: 'Here's a bite for Grandma, here's a bite for Daddy.' . . . If the family should be small and the dish of Pablum large, the list can be padded by adding the names of all the deliverymen. A friend of mine has worked out a variant of this for her little boy. With the first bite of food she says, 'Open up the garage doors, here comes the Chevy, here comes the Cadillac,' and so forth. That child took the game so seriously that eventually he would eat only foreign cars.

"Any method is better than the method I used on our first baby. In those days I believed in enthusiasm and the hard sell. . . . 'Oooh, yummy, yummy,' I would say, sounding like some manic commercial. 'Oooh, what have we got here? Tasty, tasty Pablum. Oooh, I wish I could have some of this delicious Pablum.' Then, to indicate that all was on the level, I would actually eat a spoonful or two. Even when I didn't gag, my expression would give the whole show away. In due time that baby found out who was in charge. He was."

The end of a matter is better than its beginning, and patience is better than pride.

ECCLESIASTES 7:8

TOP 10 TIPS

for Surviving Baby-hood and Beyond

In the book *Injury Time*, by English author Beryl Bainbridge, the character says, "Being constantly with children was like wearing a pair of shoes that were expensive and too small. She couldn't bear to throw them out, but they gave her blisters." Here are a few tips to help you when the blisters begin to irritate:

1. PRAY.

2. BECOME CONSCIOUS OF THE SIGNALS BETWEEN YOU AND YOUR CHILDREN THAT MEAN THINGS ARE ABOUT TO ESCALATE, AND TAKE ACTION.

3. BE CONSISTENT.

4. TRY NOT TO LET YOUR EMOTIONS RULE YOUR SPEECH AND ACTIONS.

5. PICK YOUR BATTLES WISELY.

6. USE HUMOR LIBERALLY WITH KIDS OF ANY AGE.

7. REMEMBER YOU'RE THE GROWN-UP, AND YOUR CHILDREN ARE LOOKING TO YOU TO FIND THEIR WAY.

8. TAKE INTEREST IN WHAT YOUR KIDS ARE EXPRESSING, AND VALIDATE THEIR EMOTIONS. IF THEIR RESPONSE ISN'T APPROPRIATE, GUIDE THEM IN EXPRESSING THEIR FEELINGS MORE PRODUCTIVELY.

9. TAKE CARE NOT TO BULLY YOUR KIDS.

10. INSTILL GODLY PRINCIPLES FOR LIVING INTO YOUR CHILDREN THROUGH ALL MEANS POSSIBLE, PARTICULARLY THROUGH HEARING GOD'S WORD.

CONSIDER
THIS!

We all feel confused, blue, stuck in a rut at times. It's a common human condition. The question is—is there anything we can do about it or are we all just destined to accept our bad days as inevitable?

It's easy to forget, with all the options out there for self-help, that there's an effective "guidebook" that promises to restore our courage and lighten our burdens. It's the Bible, and chances are, you already have one.

Start by reading Hebrews 4:12: "The word of God is living and active. Sharper than any double-edged sword, it penetrates even to dividing soul and spirit, joints and marrow; it judges the thoughts and attitudes of the heart." Allow the power of God's Word to brighten your day.

LIVING WORDS

A young woman was packing a suitcase for a long trip. She said to a woman who was watching her, "I'm just about finished. I only have to put in a guidebook, a lamp, a mirror, my favorite love letters, a microscope, a telescope, a volume of fine poetry, a song book, a few biographies, a package of old letters, a sword, and a set of books I have been studying." The onlooker gasped, "How do you intend to get all that in your suitcase? It's almost full now!"

The young woman replied, "Oh, all that won't take much room." She then walked over to a table, picked up her Bible, placed it in the corner of her suitcase, and closed the lid. Winking at her friend, she said, "And I even got in a loaf of living bread too."

> **WHAT IS A HOME WITHOUT A BIBLE? 'TIS A HOME WHERE DAILY BREAD FOR THE BODY IS PROVIDED, BUT THE SOUL IS NEVER FED.**
>
> CHARLES MEIGS

The Bible says of itself that it is "fresh" with every reading—it is never stale. The Bible is always applicable to life, no matter where one lives. And the truths of the Bible are unshakable—they will last forever and never go out of style. Voltaire once said that in a hundred years the Bible would be a forgotten book, found only in museums. When the hundred years were up, however, Voltaire's home was occupied by the Geneva Bible Society! Feed your children a healthy portion of the Bible today. Consider it "heavenly food."

Pay attention to what I say; listen closely to my words. Do not let them out of your sight, keep them within your heart; for they are life to those who find them.

PROVERBS 4:20-22

CERTAIN LOVE

As her daughter Janet remembers her, Jane lavished on her children the kind of love that empowered, not enslaved. She taught all four of her children how to play baseball, bake a cake, and to play fair. As Janet recalls, "She beat the living daylights out of us sometimes, and she loved us with all her heart. She taught us her favorite poets. And there is no child care in the world that will ever be a substitute for what that lady was in our lives. . . . My mother always told me to do my best, to think my best, and to do right and consider myself a person."

Another daughter, Maggy, recalls, "What gave us our self-confidence was the absolute certainty that every adult in our world loved us absolutely. They weren't always perfect, and we weren't always perfect. But we could count on that love."

Jane received love in return. Her daughter Janet declined to be considered for a job in President Clinton's administration until after her mother's death so she might remain by her ailing mother's side. When Janet Reno finally did accept a position, it was as Attorney General of the United States, the first woman to head the Justice Department.

> IF YOU WANT A BABY, HAVE A NEW ONE. DON'T BABY THE OLD ONE.
>
> JESSAMYN WEST

DISCIPLINE YOUR CHILDREN WHILE THERE IS HOPE; DO NOT SET YOUR HEART ON THEIR DESTRUCTION.

PROVERBS 19:18 NRSV

WISE WORDS

The goal of God's discipline is restoration—never condemnation. We should discipline our children with the same result in mind.

ANDREA GARNEY

No discipline seems pleasant at the time, but painful. Later on, however, it produces a harvest of righteousness and peace for those who have been trained by it.
HEBREWS 12:11

booklist

- *A Chance to Die: The Life & Legacy of Amy Carmichael*
  by Elisabeth Elliot

- *The Hiding Place & Not I, but Christ*
  by Corrie ten Boom

- *Heroes of the Holy Life: Biographies of Fully Devoted Followers of Christ*
  by Wesley Duewel

- *Unshakable Faith*
  (African American Heroes of Faith)
  by John Perry

- *Dietrich Bonhoeffer: A Biography*
  by Eberhard Bethge

FOR LOVE

PERHAPS THE MOST famous "mother" in the world is Mother Teresa. As Sister Teresa in 1948, she was given permission to leave her order of nearly twenty years and travel to India. On her first day in Calcutta, Teresa picked up five abandoned children and brought them to her "school." Before the year ended, she had forty-one students learning about hygiene in her classroom in a public park. Shortly thereafter, a new congregation was approved. Mother Teresa quickly named it "Missionaries of Charity." Within two years, their attention had turned to the care of the dying.

Once a poor beggar was picked up as he was dying in a pile of rubbish. He was reduced by suffering and hunger to a mere specter. Mother Teresa took him to the Home for the Dying and put him in bed. When she tried to wash him, she discovered his body was covered with worms. Pieces of skin came off as she washed him. For a brief moment, the man revived. In his semiconscious state, he asked, "Why do you do it?" Mother Teresa responded with the two words that are her hallmark: "For love."

Ask any mother why she does what she does, and you are likely to receive the same answer. Love is both a mother's work and a mother's reward.

> **You** reap whatever you sow.
>
> GALATIANS 6:7 NRSV

Being a full-time **mother** is one of the **highest** salaried jobs in my **field** since the **payment** is pure **love.**

MILDRED B. VERMONT

POWER OF A MOTHER'S PRAYER

Wesley L. Gustafson once related that when he was a boy—and as long as he was living at home as a young man—his mother would never go to bed until he was safely in the house. Even if he was traveling and didn't get home until near dawn, he would creep up the stairs to his room, only to find that the light was still on in his mother's room. Putting his head against the door of her room, he would hear her praying for him. Then, after he was in bed, she would come into his room. "Wes," she would call his name softly again and again.

> **Motherhood** is a partnership with God.

He would pretend to be asleep and would not respond. Feeling assured that her son was asleep, she would stand by the window and pray audibly, "O God, save my boy." Gustafson said about this, "I myself am quite sure that the prayers of a good mother never die."

Another mother, Susanna Wesley, spent one hour each day praying for her children—even though she had seventeen children for whom to care! Two of her sons are credited with bringing revival to England.

Perhaps the most beneficial thing you can do for your child is to pray for your child diligently, faithfully, daily, and with detail.

Hannah said, "For this child I prayed, and the Lord has granted me my petition which I asked of Him. Therefore I also have lent him to the Lord as long as he lives."

MILDRED B. VERMONT

✓ JUST DO IT

to do | urgent

#1

You may be someone to whom prayer comes naturally and who finds it easy to pray for your children. If not, try praying the following prayer for your children each day, as a way to begin talking with God about your kids and their lives:

#2

Almighty God, Heavenly Father, You have blessed us with the joy and care of children: Give us calm strength and patient wisdom as we bring them up, that we may teach them to love whatever is just and true and good, following the example of our Savior Jesus Christ. *Amen.*

#3

As you begin to make a habit of praying for your family, expand your prayers to include more specific requests. If you can work it in, keep a brief prayer journal to note what you've been praying on behalf of your children. You will be amazed as you see the ways in which God works through prayer.

#4

#5

#6

#7

#8

#9

#10

"The Lord can do GREAT things through those who don't care who gets the credit."

HELEN PEARSON

> **Pride lands you flat on your face; humility prepares you for honors.**
>
> PROVERBS 29:23 MSG

DETERMINED COMPASSION

One night in 1837, she believed she heard the voice of God informing her that she had a mission. Nine years later, that mission began to take shape when a friend sent her information about the Institution of Protestant Deaconesses in Germany. She later entered that institution to learn how to care for the sick. In 1853 she became superintendent of a "woman's hospital" in London. But then the Crimean War broke out in 1854, and she volunteered at once to care for British soldiers, leaving for Constantinople almost immediately.

Once in Turkey, she was given charge of the nursing at the military hospital. Even though doctors were hostile toward her and the hospital itself was deplorably filthy, she dug in her heels and began caring for her patients, at first using the provisions she had brought with her and then undertaking a correspondence campaign to resupply the hospital. She spent many hours each day in the wards, touching virtually every man who ever entered the hospital. The comfort she gave on night rounds earned her the nickname "The Lady with the Lamp."

Her selfless giving eventually made her name synonymous with compassionate nursing care—her name was Florence Nightingale.

Who's Who:

Ruth

The book of Ruth relates the story of a young woman who displayed a fierce loyalty to her mother-in-law, and later on, to her people, the Hebrews. When Ruth's husband died, her mother-in-law Naomi urged her to leave and return to her own people. Ruth refused, and determined to stay with Naomi, saying, "Where you go I will go, and where you stay I will stay. Your people will be my people and your God my God. Where you die I will die, and there I will be buried. May the LORD deal with me, be it ever so severely, if anything but death separates you and me" (1:16,17). Ruth thought only of the welfare of Naomi.

There was no apparent advantage to young Ruth staying with her mother-in-law. Ruth's devotion was known among the people where they lived, and Ruth was esteemed in many ways because of it. The LORD blessed Ruth, and Naomi through her. When Ruth married a prominent man in their community, Boaz, God blessed them with a son, whom they named Obed. The women around Naomi said to her, "Praise be to the LORD, who this day has not left you without a kinsman-redeemer. May he become famous throughout Israel. He will renew your life and sustain you in your old age. For your daughter-in-law, who loves you and who is better to you than seven sons, has given him birth" (4:14-15). He did become famous. Obed was the father of Jesse, the father of the great King David and the direct lineage of Christ.

All of this good from the absolutely selfless devotion of one woman to another. There is great power and promise in acting with determined, selfless sacrifice.

GETTING THEIR ATTENTION

TERESA BLOOMINGDALE offers these humorous suggestions for improving family communication:

1. If you have tiny children who won't give you their attention, simply place a long- distance telephone call to somebody important, preferably their grandmother. Your toddlers will immediately climb up on your lap and become all ears.

2. If you have older children who avoid you like the plague, buy yourself some expensive bath salts, run a hot tub, and settle in. . . . Teenagers who haven't talked to you since their tenth birthday will bang on the door, demanding your immediate attention.

3. Lure your husband into the bedroom and lock the door. The entire family will immediately converge in the hallway, insisting they must talk to you.

4. Get a job in an office that discourages personal phone calls. Your kids will then call you every hour on the hour.

5. Send them away to college, or let them move into an apartment. They can then be counted on . . . for long chats, during which they will expound at length on what wonderful parents you were, and what happened, because you certainly are spoiling their younger siblings rotten.

lighten up

A second grader came home from school and said to her mother, "Mom, guess what? We learned how to make babies today."

The mother, more than a little surprised, tried to keep her cool. "That's interesting," she said, "How do you make babies?"

"It's simple," her daughter replied. "You just change the 'y' to 'i' and add 'es'."

God will yet fill your mouth with laughter . . .

The quickest way for a **parent** to get a child's attention is to sit down and **look comfortable.**

LANE OLINHOUSE

and your lips with joyful shouting. JOB 8:21 AMP

THE BRIGHTEST MINDS

> **NEVER** DESPAIR OF A **CHILD.** THE ONE YOU **WEEP** THE MOST FOR AT THE MERCYSEAT MAY **FILL** YOUR **HEART** WITH THE SWEETEST **JOYS.**
>
> T.L. CUYLER

A PARTIALLY deaf boy came home from school one day carrying a note from officials at the school. The note suggested that the parents take the boy out of school, claiming that he was "too stupid to learn."

The boy's mother read the note and said, "My son Tom isn't 'too stupid to learn.' I'll teach him myself." And so she did.

When Tom died many years later, the people of the United States of America paid tribute to him by turning off the nation's lights for one full minute. You see, this Tom had invented the light bulb—and not only that, but motion pictures and the record player. In all, he had more than one thousand patents to his credit.

No child is beyond learning more than they know today. No child is beyond finding a new way to express their creativity and their love.

No child is beyond receiving affection and growing in self-esteem. No child is beyond experiencing the presence of Almighty God.

Never give up on any aspect of your child's growth and development. Your Heavenly Father hasn't, doesn't, and won't.

He who goes out weeping,
carrying seed to sow, will return with songs of
joy, carrying sheaves with him.

PSALM 126:6

TOP **10** TIPS for Guiding Your Child's Education

1. EXPLORE ALL THE SCHOOL OPTIONS AVAILABLE TO MEET THE SPECIAL INTERESTS AND NEEDS OF YOUR CHILD.

2. PRAY FOR WISDOM THAT GOD WILL GUIDE YOU AND YOUR CHILD TOWARD THE RIGHT CLASSROOM.

3. BE INVOLVED IN YOUR CHILD'S EDUCATION. VOLUNTEER IN THE CLASSROOM. VISIT SCHOOL WEB SITES. TALK WITH OTHER PARENTS.

4. TALK WITH YOUR CHILD'S TEACHER IF YOU SEE A PROBLEM.

5. DON'T HESITATE TO HAVE YOUR CHILD EVALUATED IF YOU SUSPECT A LEARNING DISABILITY OR SPECIAL NEED.

6. PLACE SCHOOL AND LEARNING IN A POSITIVE LIGHT, AND ENCOURAGE OLDER SIBLINGS TO DO THE SAME FOR YOUNGER ONES.

7. SHARE IN THE LEARNING. HELP BRING EXCITEMENT TO TOPICS YOU CAN EXPLORE TOGETHER.

8. INTRODUCE YOUR CHILD TO THE LIBRARY AND OTHER METHODS OF RESEARCHING EARLY.

9. TAKE YOUR CHILD TO MUSEUMS, CONCERTS, LOCAL FAIRS, AND EVENTS THAT WILL EXPOSE THEM TO ARTS, MUSIC, NATURE, AND SCIENCE.

10. EXPLORE THE SPIRITUAL ASPECT OF LIFE AS WELL THROUGH CHURCH AND BIBLE READING TOGETHER.

CONSIDER THIS!

Do you allow room in your busy life for quiet—to hear your own thoughts, to truly listen to others, to discern the voice of God? Noise pervades the life of a mother. It seems that children have two levels of volume: loud and louder. Many of today's "toys" can only be called sadistic, with off-the-charts decibel levels and noises that no human could ever make. Then there are TVs, phones, and stereos.

In Scripture, the Lord says, "Be still and know that I am God" (Psalm 46:10). Make time for quiet each day, even if for a few minutes. Allow for silence in your home, if at all possible. This practice can help you to gather thoughts and allow you to hear what God has to say to your heart. It also lets your kids know that it's okay if nobody's talking.

LANGUAGE IN SILENCE

Author and pastor's wife Colleen Townsend Evans has written, "Silence need not be awkward or embarrassing, for to be with one you love, without the need for words, is a beautiful and satisfying form of communication.

A MOTHER UNDERSTANDS WHAT A CHILD DOES NOT SAY.

"I remember times when our children used to come running to me, all of them chattering at once about the events of their day— and it was wonderful to have them share their feelings with me. But there were also the times when they came to me wanting only to be held, to have me stroke their heads and caress them into sleep. And so it is, sometimes, with us and with God our Father."

Don't force your child to talk to you. Give them the respect and "space" to remain silent. Sometimes children need to work out their own ideas and opinions in quiet before voicing them. On the other hand, when they do talk, take time to listen intently, carefully, and kindly. In so doing, your child will know that they can talk to you whenever they want or need to, and you can rest assured that their silence is not rooted in suspicion or fear of you.

The language of silence is a language.

Serve God with wholehearted devotion and with a willing mind, for the LORD searches every heart and understands every motive behind the thoughts.

1 CHRONICLES 28:9

WOMAN OF STRENGTH

Lech Walesa, the first freely elected president of Poland in fifty years and the 1983 winner of the Nobel Prize for Peace, credits his mother for teaching him the values that led to his success. He writes about her in his book, *Lech Walesa: A Way of Hope,* "She is the only person from my childhood I still have a really clear recollection of. She took an interest in history and current affairs, and read a great deal. In the evenings, she would sometimes read to us. We took great pleasure in these moments. All the stories our mother told us had a moral in them: they taught one to be honest, to strive always to better oneself, to be just, and to call white white and black black. Mother was very religious. My faith can be said almost to have flowed into me with my mother's milk."

> ALL THAT I AM OR HOPE TO BE, I OWE TO MY MOTHER.
> ABRAHAM LINCOLN

The children in the Walesa home were kept on a "tight rein," he recalls. Even the youngest had jobs to do—tending geese, taking the cows out to pasture, doing a variety of manual jobs.

Wisdom, faith, and discipline all have a mother's knee as their first foundation—and what a strong and wonderful foundation it can be if the mother is a woman who seeks those same qualities in her own life!

GET ALL THE ADVICE YOU CAN AND BE WISE THE REST OF YOUR LIFE.

PROVERBS 19:20 TLB

WISE WORDS

A good woman is hard to find,
And worth far more than diamonds. . . .
She always faces tomorrow with a smile.
When she speaks she has something worthwhile to say,
And she always says it kindly.
She keeps an eye on everyone in her household,
And keeps them all busy and productive.
Her children respect and bless her;
Her husband joins in with words of praise:
"Many women have done wonderful things,
but you've outclassed them all!"
Charm can mislead and beauty soon fades.
The woman to be admired and praised
Is the woman who lives in the Fear-of-God.
Give her everything she deserves!
Festoon her life with praises!

PROVERBS 31:10,25-31 MSG

booklist

tips for getting your children to and through college

- *Parent's Guide to College Admissions*
  by Marjorie Nieuwenhuis

- *The Parent's Financial Survival Guide*
  by Theodore Hughes, David Klein

- *Total Money Makeover: A Proven Plan for Financial Fitness*
  by Dave Ramsey

- *Money Matters Workbook for Teens, Ages 15-18*
  by Larry Burkett

- *The Burkett and Blue Definitive Guide to Securing Wealth to Last*
  by Larry Burkett, Ron Blue

SURVIVING WITH KIDS

A COLLEGE FRESHMAN once wrote the following to her parents:

Dear Mom and Dad,

Just thought I'd drop you a note to clue you in on my plans. I've fallen in love with a guy named Buck. He quit high school between his sophomore and junior year to travel with his motorcycle gang. He was married at eighteen and had two sons. About a year ago he got a divorce.

We've been going steady for two months now and plan to get married in the fall. (He thinks he should be able to find a job by then.) Until then, I've decided to move into his apartment. I think I might be pregnant.

At any rate, I dropped out of school last week. I was just bored with the whole thing. Maybe I'll finish college sometime in the future.

[And then on the next page she continued . . .]

Mom and Dad, everything I've written so far in this letter is false. NONE OF IT IS TRUE! But, Mom and Dad, it IS true that I got a C in French and flunked my math test. And it IS true that I'm overdrawn and need more money for my tuition payments.

Your loving daughter.

> **I shall** be joyful in the Lord.
>
> PSALM 35:9 AMP

Children are a great comfort in your old age—and they help you reach it faster, too.

LIONEL M. KAUFMAN

Pray without ceasing.

1 THESSALONIANS 5:17 KJV

GIVING, BODY & SOUL

The actor known as Mr. T. gave an unusual tribute to his mother. He said that he wanted to recognize "her hands, her feet, and her knees."

He called attention to his mother's feet because they had taken her across town to do domestic work—her hands and knees used to scrub floors and toilets. He also said, "She used her feet to walk against my sickness when my body was ill and racked with pain. It was my mother who walked the floor with me, on her feet all night long, talking to God; then she would get down on her knees to pray some more, still holding me in her hands." He adds, "I guess the only payment she ever wanted was for me to grow up and carry on her teachings . . . to share, to love, to be kind and always take God with me wherever I go. . . . She always said, 'Don't be bitter, don't hate, don't hold grudges, and never forget to pray.'

"It's so hard to try to describe my mother's endurance, her patience, her love, her feelings for her family, her spiritual convictions, her right to be, her loyalty and her pride in parenthood. I will just say that my mother was God-sent."

Feet to walk, hands to carry, knees to bend in prayer. What a legacy for any mother to give a child!

Who's Who:

Elijah

Elijah is known as the Prophet of Fire—and as the only human ever to have been taken into heaven without experiencing death. Elijah was also dedicated to earnest prayer.

The apostle James, in writing about prayer, illustrates his message by saying, "Elijah was a man just like us. He prayed earnestly that it would not rain, and it did not rain on the land for three and a half years. Again he prayed, and the heavens gave rain, and the earth produced its crops" (James 5:17, 18).

Elijah spoke to God with honesty, baring his heart and thoughts before his Creator. God honored that by revealing His character and nature to Elijah and enabling him to perform miracles. Elijah's life and work were characterized by earnest, forthright prayer and the belief that God would hear and answer.

DIVINE PURPOSE

DR. WALTER L. WILSON tells the story of a woman who attended one of his meetings. She waited after the service so she could have a few private moments with him since she felt as if her life had no meaning and no purpose—that she was invisible to God. As part of his counseling, Dr. Wilson asked the woman if she could quote any of the Scriptures. She replied that she had once learned John 3:16 in Sunday school.

Dr. Wilson then asked the woman to recite the verse. She said, "For God so loved the world, that he gave his only forgotten Son, that whosoever believeth in him should not perish, but have everlasting life."

Immediately Dr. Wilson noticed that she had used the word forgotten instead of begotten in quoting the verse. He asked, "Do you know why God forgot His Son?" She said, "No, I don't." He replied, "It was because He wanted to remember you."

Apart from your personal and family reasons for bearing your child, the Lord has a divine reason for your child's birth. He has a place for your child to fill and a role for your child to fulfill. Every child is planned and wanted from God's perspective!

> **There's a time** when you have to explain to your children why they're born, and it's a marvelous thing if you know the reason.
>
> HAZEL SCOT

The LORD said, "Before I formed
you in the womb I knew you;
before you were born, I sanctified you."

JEREMIAH 1:5 NKJV

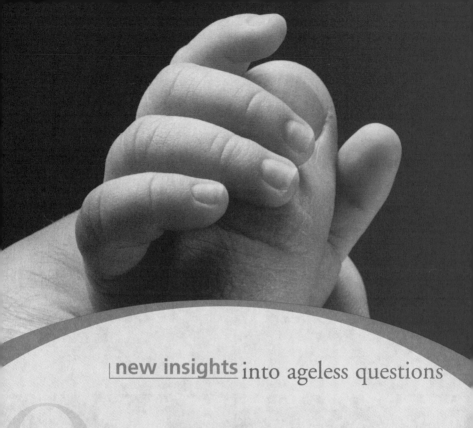

new insights into ageless questions

I know the Bible says God loves me, but I still have trouble feeling like He really cares about me. How can I know for sure?

Throughout Scripture, God has given us many ways to know that He values and loves His children, starting right from the beginning. Genesis 1:26 says that God created men and women in His own image and likeness and gave them dominion over all the earth. When humans sinned and turned away from God, time and again, God expressed a desire to have humankind reconciled to Him. And then, in the ultimate gesture of love, God made the way through the sacrifice and resurrection of Jesus Christ.

When you begin to doubt God's love, remember what Paul said to the Ephesian Christians: I pray "that you, being rooted and grounded in love, may be able to comprehend with all the saints what is the width and length and depth and height—to know the love of Christ which passes knowledge; that you may be filled with all the fullness of God" (Ephesians 3:14-19 NKJV).

Fun Trivia

Who did Luke describe as "one of the daughters of Aaron," meaning that she was descended through the priestly line? She was also married to a priest. Her name means "God is my oath." Who was her rather unusual son? Read Luke 1:5-80.

Who was commended in scripture for her spiritual influence over her son? Her name means "conquering well." Though she was a Jewess, she married a Gentile. Who was her evangelist son? Read Acts 16:1-3; 2 Timothy 1:5; 3:14-15; 4:5.

What Old Testament woman became the mother of a king—who the Bible says "did that which was right in the sight of the Lord"? Her name means "darling of Jehovah." Even though he had a wicked father, this mother influenced her son to follow God. How old was her son when he became king? Read 2 Kings 22:1, 2.

Answers: 1: Elizabeth and John the Baptist; 2: Eunice and Timothy; 3: Jedidah, her son Josiah was 8 years old when he became king. He reigned for 31 years.

CHILD IN NEED

Children **need** love,
especially when they
do not **deserve** it.

Humorist Erma Bombeck once wrote: "Every mother has a favorite child. She cannot help it. She is only human. I have mine—the child for whom I feel a special closeness, with whom I share a love that no one else could possibly understand. My favorite child is the one who was too sick to eat ice cream at his birthday party . . . who had measles at Christmas . . . who wore leg braces to bed because he toed in . . . who had a fever in the middle of the night, the asthma attack, the child in my arms at the emergency ward.

"My favorite child is the one who messed up the piano recital, misspelled committee in a spelling bee, ran the wrong way with the football, and had his bike stolen because he was careless.

"My favorite child was selfish, immature, bad-tempered and self-centered. He was vulnerable, lonely, unsure of what he was doing in this world—and quite wonderful.

"All mothers have their favorite child. It is always the same one: the one who needs you at the moment. Who needs you for whatever reason—to cling to, to shout at, to hurt, to hug, to flatter, to reverse charges to, to unload on—but mostly just to be there."

[Jesus said,]
"Be merciful, just as
your Father
also is merciful."

LUKE 6:36 NKJV

NIGHTTIME STRATEGY

> PEOPLE WHO **SAY** THEY **SLEEP** LIKE A **BABY** USUALLY **DON'T** HAVE **ONE.**
>
> LEO J. BURKE

KATHY AND JIM were longing for the day when their precious baby would eventually sleep all the way through the night. Originally they had agreed to take turns getting up when she cried. But Jim frequently gave in to the urge to prompt his wife into taking his turn by saying, "Honey, she's probably hungry." That, of course, was a problem only a nursing mother could address.

Their fatigue, however, was greatly mitigated by the considerable joy they had in watching little Anna grow and gain new skills, not the least of which was her attempt at learning to talk.

Even though she knew that most babies have "Mama" as their first word, Kathy felt her beloved husband would be thrilled if Anna's first word was for him. So, day after day, she worked with her bright baby to teach her to say what she was sure would be a magical word to her daddy's ears.

One night, all of Kathy's diligence paid off. At 2:15 A.M., Anna awoke and cried "Da-da" at the top of her lungs. Kathy turned over and said softly to her husband beside her, "She's calling for you, dear, and I'm sure this is something only you can handle."

A **cheerful** disposition is **good** for your **health.**

PROVERBS 17:22 MSG

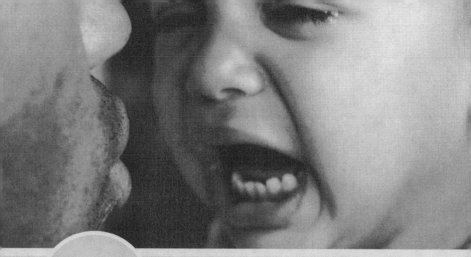

TOP **10** TIPS for Getting Enough Rest

1. CATCH NAPS WHEN YOUR CHILD IS NAPPING.

2. SIT DOWN ONCE IN A WHILE, AND PUT YOUR FEET UP.

3. ESTABLISH A BEDTIME ROUTINE AND TIME, SO YOUR CHILD KNOWS WHAT TO EXPECT.

4. TALK WITH YOUR SPOUSE TO PLAN TIMES WHEN YOU CAN COUNT ON GETTING SOME SLEEP.

5. IF ANXIETY IS KEEPING YOU FROM SLEEP, PRAY THAT GOD WILL HELP YOU RELEASE YOUR WORRY AND GIVE YOU TRULY RESTFUL SLEEP.

6. IF YOU CAN, GO TO BED WHEN YOUR KIDS DO AT LEAST ONCE A WEEK.

7. TRY TO GET EXERCISE DURING THE DAY. REGULAR EXERCISE HAS BEEN PROVEN TO LEAD TO BETTER SLEEP.

8. KNOW WHEN IT'S TIME TO STOP GETTING UP WITH YOUR KIDS DURING THE NIGHT.

9. WORK ON HAVING SOME DOWNTIME FOR YOURSELF PRIOR TO BEDTIME.

10. VALUE REST. THERE'S NO VIRTUE IN BEING EXHAUSTED BECAUSE YOU TAKE ON TOO MUCH OR DON'T ALLOW YOURSELF TO RELAX.

CONSIDER
THIS!

Do you realize that in this world we are all born as orphans, separated from God's family? In His incredible love, grace, and mercy, He made a way for each person to become adoptive children, restored to family status again. Scripture says: "To all who received him, to those who believed in his name, he gave the right to become children of God—children born not of natural descent, nor of human decision or a husband's will, but born of God" (John 1:12-13).

Open your heart and your home to those little ones who need to experience love—the same love God has shown to you.

LOVE CHANGES THINGS

Stephanie was orphaned after both of her parents died. With no other relatives to care for her, she was put into foster care. Eventually she came to live with the Weavers. Mrs. Weaver found Stephanie sullen, withdrawn, and uncommunicative. She asked to see her records. The first foster family wrote, "Stephanie is a quiet, shy girl." The second family wrote, "She obeys, but she doesn't participate much in the family." Mrs. Weaver thought, *I doubt if Stephanie will be with us long.* Still, she decided to keep Stephanie through the Christmas holiday and then talk to her social worker about a transfer to another home.

> A LITTLE BOY'S MOTHER ONCE TOLD HIM THAT IT IS GOD WHO MAKES PEOPLE GOOD. HE LOOKED UP AND REPLIED, "YES, I KNOW IT IS GOD, BUT MOTHERS HELP A LOT."

At Christmas, the Weavers exchanged a number of lovely presents, including gifts for Stephanie. Then Stephanie handed Mrs. Weaver a brown paper sack with a rough drawing of a Christmas scene on it. She opened it to find a rhinestone necklace with a couple of stones missing and a little bottle of perfume, half empty. As she put on the necklace and dabbed perfume behind her ear, Stephanie said, "Mom's necklace looks good on you. You smell good like she did too." Mrs. Weaver's heart melted. She vowed to renew her efforts to love Stephanie, and she succeeded! By the following Christmas, Stephanie had become her adopted daughter.

Reject not nor forsake the teaching of your mother.

PROVERBS 1:8 AMP

LIFE-GIVING SACRIFICE

A number of years ago, a young mother was making her way on foot across the hills of South Wales, carrying her tiny baby in her arms. The wintry winds were stronger than she anticipated and her journey took much longer than planned. Eventually, she was overtaken by a blinding blizzard.

> MOTHER MEANS SELFLESS DEVOTION, LIMITLESS SACRIFICE, AND LOVE THAT PASSES UNDERSTANDING.

The woman never reached her destination. When the blizzard had subsided, those expecting her arrival went in search of her. After hours of searching, they finally found her body underneath a mound of snow.

As they shoveled the snow away from her frozen corpse, they were amazed to see that she had taken off her outer clothing. When they finally lifted her body away from the ground, they discovered the reason why. This brave and self-sacrificing young mother had wrapped her own cloak and scarf around her baby and then huddled over her child. When the searchers unwrapped the child, they found to their great surprise and joy that he was alive and well!

Years later, that child, David Lloyd George, became prime minister of Great Britain and is regarded as one of England's greatest statesmen.

[JESUS SAID,] "NO ONE HAS GREATER LOVE THAN THIS, TO LAY DOWN ONE'S LIFE FOR ONE'S FRIENDS."

JOHN 15:13 NRSV

WiSE WoRDS

A mother's love for the child
of her body differs essentially
from all other affections,
and burns with so steady and
clear a flame that it appears
like the one unchangeable
thing in this earthly mutable
life, so that when she is no
longer present it is still a
light to our steps and a con-
solation.

W. H. HUDSON

booklist

THE GIFTS OF HOSPITALITY

A BUSINESSMAN CALLED his wife one day to get her permission for him to bring home a visiting foreigner as a dinner guest that night. At the time, the wife had three children in school and one preschooler at home, so she had a full workload on any given day, apart from entertaining strangers. Still, she consented, and the meal she prepared was both delicious and graciously served. The foreigner, an important official in Spain, had a delightful time and thanked the couple repeatedly for inviting him into their home and treating him to a home-cooked meal and an evening of family warmth and fellowship.

> **A man's** work is from sun to sun, but a mother's work is never done.

Years later, friends of this family went to Spain as missionaries. Their work was brought to a standstill, however, by government regulations. This particular Spanish official got word that the missionaries were friends of the couple who had hosted him in such a loving manner, and he used his influence to clear away the restrictions on their behalf. A church exists today in that province of Spain, due in part to the setting of one extra place at one dinner table!

As busy as you may be today, take time for the people God may bring across your path. Who knows what plan God may have for both of your futures.

Her lamp does not go out at night.

PROVERBS 31:18 NRSV

SPINNING YOUR WHEELS

A philosophical clock—one capable of deep pondering and meditation—once spent a great deal of time thinking about its own future. It reasoned that it had to tick twice each second. *How much ticking might that be?* the clock questioned.

The clock calculated that it would tick 120 times each minute, which was 7,200 times every hour. In the twenty-four hours of a day it would tick 172,800 times. This meant 63,072,000 times every year. By this time, the clock had begun to perspire profusely at the very thought.

> **Worry is like** a rocking chair: It gives you something to do, but doesn't get you anywhere.

Finally the clock calculated that in a ten-year period it would have to tick 630,720,000 times—and at that point the clock collapsed from nervous exhaustion.

An equally scientific and philosophical person has concluded that ninety-five percent of all that we worry about happening—doesn't. Of the five percent that does happen, four out of five times things turn out much better than anticipated, including a few outright blessings! In the end, only one percent of all the bad that we think might happen actually does, and of this it's rarely as bad as feared. So, in the words of a Bobby McFarrin song, "Don't worry! Be happy!"

Casting the whole of your care [all your anxieties, all your worries, all your concerns, once and for all] on Him, for He cares for you affectionately and cares about you watchfully.

1 PETER 5:7 AMP

When you feel overwhelmed by worry, try this burden-lifting exercise. On an index card, write the following prayer:

Lord, I'm worried about _____ right now, and I'm having trouble giving this over to You. Please help me to have the strength of will to let this go, so I can serve You unencumbered by this weight. I thank You for what You are going to do regarding this matter. Amen.

Read the prayer, mentally putting the name of the person or circumstance in the blank. Carry the card with you in your purse or diaper bag, but keep it to yourself. Just a little contract between you and your God. After awhile, you won't need the card; you'll be able to recite the prayer from memory, and you will be in the habit of releasing your cares to God.

"A house without love may be a CASTLE, or a palace, but it is not a home; love is the life of a true home."

JOHN LUBBOCK

TRUE LIFE OF HOME

Women are often tempted to think that their homemaking skills—such as cooking, decorating, cleaning—are what turn a house into a home. But consider how one of the most famous cooks of all time, Julia Child, recalls her own childhood:

"I know I'm happy. I was very fortunate in my family background because I had a very loving, supportive family. We had no conflict. My sister was five years younger; and we had a brother halfway between, so we never had any sibling rivalry. My parents were happy; we were not rich, but comfortably well-off. My mother thought everything we did was absolutely marvelous.

"I think your background makes an awful lot of difference. I don't know what you do if you've been abused, or haven't been praised enough so that you don't feel that you're okay. I was very fortunate in having such a happy background. I was never brilliant in school, but I never had any problems either, so I didn't feel inferior. I did have the problem of being twice as tall as anyone else, but that didn't seem to make any difference because my mother always said we were so wonderful, no matter what."

Notice Julia didn't make one mention of her mother's cooking skills or food, only of praise!

Who's Who:

Lavina Christensen Fugal

Lavina Christensen Fugal knew the key to being a good mother. Others noticed, too, and in 1955 Lavina had the distinguished honor of being voted American Mother of the Year. She said this about raising children (she raised eight of her own): "Love your children with all your hearts, love them enough to discipline them before it is too late. Praise them for important things, even if you have to stretch them a bit. Praise them a lot. They live on it like bread and butter and they need it more than bread and butter."

Lavina's special gift for nurturing and encouragement were also extended to those in her community. Many residents of Pleasant Grove, Utah, referred to her as "Aunt Lavina."

The Bible seems to commend Lavina further with these words in 2 Timothy 4:2: "Be prepared in season and out of season; correct, rebuke and encourage—with great patience and careful instruction." These are words every mother can take to heart.

UTILITY COMMANDMENTS

Parents have a few habits that children never seem to understand, or to copy—such as flipping off lights in rooms with no one in them and turning off faucets in a bathroom. In *Family: The Ties That Bind—and Gag!* author Erma Bombeck offers these "Commandments for the Utilities:"

1. Thou shalt flush. Especially if thou is fifteen years old and has the use of both arms.

2. Thou shalt hang up the phone when thou has been on it long enough for the rates to change.

3. Thou shalt not stand in front of the refrigerator door waiting for something to dance.

4. Thou shalt not covet the rest of the family's hot water.

5. Thou shalt honor thy father's and mother's thermostat and keep it on normal.

6. Thou shalt remember last month's electricity bill and rejoice in darkness.

7. Unfortunately, notes Bombeck, these commandments generally lay in a family like broken stone tablets amidst wet towels and melting soap!

lighten up

You Know You're a Mom When...

- You hide in the bathroom to be alone.
- You have time to shave only one leg at a time.
- Your child throws up and you catch it.
- You cling to the high moral ground on toy weapons but your child chews his toast into the shape of a gun.
- You hope ketchup is a vegetable, since it's the only one your child eats.
- You have no qualms about cleaning your child's face with saliva.
- You can't bear to give away baby clothes—it's so final.
- You've mastered the skill of putting food on a plate without letting anything touch.
- You wonder if you're cut out for this "mom" assignment, but you wouldn't trade it for anything.

I shall be
joyful
in the
Lord.

PSALM 35:9 AMP

see a child under twelve turn off an electric light?

"CONTROLLED" CHAOS

Harriet Rukenbrod Day's poem "A Mother's Dilemma" says it well:

Baby's in the cookie jar
Sister's in the glue
Kitty's in the birdie's cage
And I am in a stew!
Time for dad to come to lunch
Someone's spilled the roses
Breakfast dishes still undone
The twins have drippy noses.
Junior has the stove apart
Dinner guests at eight
Neighbors' kids swoop in like flies
How can I concentrate?
Telephone keeps ringing wildly
Someone's in the hall
Fido's chewed the rug to bits
The preacher's come to call!
Would mothers like to chuck their load?
They couldn't stand the rap
Easy, mild existences
Would cause their nerves to snap!

> **If evolution** really works, how come mothers have only two hands?
>
> ED DUSSAULT

The joy of the LORD is your strength.

NEHEMIAH 8:10 KJV

TOP **10** TIPS

for Coping with Chaos

1. START THE DAY BY TALKING TO GOD.

2. TAKE TIME EVERY DAY FOR TIME ALONE READING, TAKING A WALK, OR HAVING A HOT CUP OF JAVA.

3. BREATHE. IT SOUNDS SILLY, BUT MANY PEOPLE DEALING WITH STRESSFUL SITUATIONS TAKE SHALLOW BREATHS OR EVEN HOLD THEIR BREATH.

4. DRINK PLENTY OF WATER AND PAY ATTENTION TO WHAT YOU'RE EATING—DEHYDRATION AND LOW BLOOD SUGAR SAP ENERGY AND CAN LEAD TO SERIOUS HEALTH PROBLEMS.

5. KNOW YOUR LIMITS—AND LIMIT WHAT YOU TAKE ON.

6. REMIND YOURSELF THAT THE WILDLY CHAOTIC TIMES WITH YOUR KIDS WILL PASS.

7. STAY LOOSE, AND ADJUST EXPECTATIONS AS YOU GO ALONG. SOME DAYS, IF YOU GET THE KIDS AND YOURSELF FED, YOU CAN CONSIDER YOUR JOB WELL DONE.

8. DON'T ISOLATE YOURSELF. MAKE TIME TO GET TOGETHER WITH FRIENDS.

9. KEEP COMMUNICATION OPEN WITH YOUR SPOUSE, AND TALK WITH HIM ABOUT WHERE AND WHEN YOU NEED HIM TO PITCH IN.

10. ENJOY THE NOISE AND EXCITEMENT THAT KIDS INEVITABLY BRING TO YOUR LIFE—SOMEDAY THE HOUSE WILL BE QUIET AND ORDERLY, AND A PART OF YOU WILL LONG FOR THESE TIMES.

CONSIDER THIS!

Throughout the Bible, God has taken care to give His children promises and reassurance that He is our devoted Heavenly Father in whom we can trust. Hebrews 13:5-6 reads, "God has said, 'Never will I leave you; never will I forsake you.' So we say with confidence, 'The Lord is my helper; I will not be afraid. What can man do to me?'"

God knows that His children need these words, need to know the character and trustworthiness of His nature, need to know that we can depend on Him.

In the same way, your children need to see that you are available to them. They need to see your character and be assured that they can trust in and rely on you. This provides the basis for their security in life and ultimately, their faith in God.

KNOWING YOU'RE THERE

In 1971, child-care expert Penelope Leach had a crisis that changed her life, and also many of her opinions about the needs and growth of children. Leach was well launched into a promising career as a child-development researcher when her two-year-old son, Matthew, nearly died of viral meningitis. While allowing her time to care for her sick child, Leach's employer also pressed her to return to work as quickly as possible. So as soon as Matthew was out of danger, Leach left him with a babysitter and returned to her job. She says, "I just took it for granted that's what I had to do."

Physically, Matthew was well, but Leach found that "you could

> **TOO MUCH LOVE NEVER SPOILS CHILDREN. CHILDREN BECOME SPOILED WHEN WE SUBSTITUTE "PRESENTS" FOR "PRESENCE."**
>
> DR. ANTHONY P. WITHAM

reduce him to tears playing peekaboo. The only person he was okay with was me." So, two months later, Leach made another decision—this time to quit her job and devote herself to the "total health" of her child. Today, she looks back with embarrassment that she ever allowed her son to reach such a low point in his emotional growth. She recalls, "Quitting was tough, but it wasn't as if we were going to starve." What didn't happen as the result of her quitting was that Matthew didn't starve for the assurance, comfort, attention, and love he needed.

We loved you so much that we were delighted to share with you not only the gospel of God but our lives as well, because you had become so dear to us.

1 THESSALONIANS 2:8

ETERNAL INFLUENCE

Whenever I held my newborn baby in my arms," Rose once said, "I used to think that what I said and did to him could have an influence not only on him but on all whom he met, not only for a day or a month or a year, but for all eternity—a very, very challenging and exciting thought for a mother." Feeling this duty, Rose became a natural and determined teacher of her children, leading them by discovery, story, example, and inspiration to fulfill their own destinies.

Rose engaged her children in conversation about history and politics, and when guests visited their home, she expected her children to ask questions and offer opinions. Even though the family was wealthy, the boys were expected to fix their own bicycles and were required to earn their own pocket money. She gave each child a sense of independence and privacy, yet dressed them with similar clothes so they would feel a part of a whole family unit. Rose expected her children to be self-confident adults and independent thinkers, with compassion for those less fortunate.

And she succeeded. Among Rose Kennedy's children, son John became President of the United States, son Robert, Attorney General, and son Edward, a United States Senator.

> A MOTHER IS NOT A PERSON TO LEAN ON, BUT A PERSON TO MAKE LEANING UNNECESSARY.
>
> DOROTHY CANFIELD FISHER

A MAN LEAVES HIS FATHER AND MOTHER AND IS JOINED TO HIS WIFE, AND THE TWO ARE UNITED INTO ONE.

GENESIS 2:24 NLT

WISE WORDS

A Mother's Creed

- I believe in the eternal importance of the home as the fundamental institution of society.
- I believe in the immeasurable possibilities of every boy and girl.
- I believe in the imagination, the trust, the hopes, and the ideals which dwell in the hearts of all children.
- I believe in the beauty of nature, of art, of books, and of friendship.
- I believe in the satisfaction of duty.
- I believe in the little homely joys of everyday life.
- I believe in the goodness of the great design which lies behind our complex world.
- I believe in the safety and peace that surround us all through the overbrooding love of God.

OZORA DAVIS

booklist

read more about it...trusting god

- *Why? Trusting God When You Don't Understand*
  by Anne Graham Lotz

- *Trusting God: Even When Life Hurts*
  by Jerry Bridges

- *Courageous Faith: Trusting God When Times Are Tough*
  by Keith Bower

- *Life on the Edge: Trusting God When Things Go Wrong*
  by James C. Dobson

- *Trusting God's Heart: Finding Peace in Times of Sorrow*
  by Dr. Frank Cox

LOOKING ABOVE

J.C. PENNEY WAS WELL advanced in years before he committed his life fully to Jesus Christ. A good, honest man, he was primarily interested in his early years in becoming a success and making money. As a clerk working for six dollars a week at Joslin's Dry Goods Store in Denver, he had an ambition to one day be worth one hundred thousand dollars. When he reached that goal he felt temporary satisfaction, but soon set his sights on being worth a million dollars.

Both Mr. and Mrs. Penney worked hard to expand their business, but one day Mrs. Penney caught cold and developed pneumonia, which subsequently caused her death. "When she died," J. C. recalled, "my world crashed about me. To build a business, to make a success in the eyes of men, to accumulate money—what was the purpose of life? . . . I felt mocked by life, even by God himself." Before long, Penney was ruined financially and in deep distress. It was at that point that he turned to God and experienced a true spiritual conversion. He said, "When I was brought to humility and the knowledge of dependence on God, sincerely and earnestly seeking God's aid, it was forthcoming, and a light illumined my being. I cannot otherwise describe it than to say that it changed me as a man."

Jesus gives meaning and purpose to life. He brings calm to the storm. He brings rest to the soul.

> **Look around you** and be distressed, look within you and be depressed, look to Jesus and be at rest.

Looking unto *Jesus* the author and finisher of our faith.

HEBREWS 12:2 KJV

"A sweater is a garment worn BY A CHILD when his mother feels chilly."

BARBARA JOHNSON

CHOOSING WISELY

Eight-year-old William was appreciative but not enthusiastic when he found skis under the Christmas tree. They had not been high on his wish list, but his father knew he would need them for an upcoming family trip.

As it turned out, the skis were the best gift he ever received. William took to the sport his first day on the slopes, and he joined the resort's junior racer program. For the next ten years, William skied every winter weekend, sometimes getting up in subzero cold to be at the mountain early. The skis taught him self-discipline and persistence. He learned to get up after falling hard. At home, he learned to budget his time to allow for homework. William became a hard-working, focused young adult willing to dare because he wasn't afraid to fail. The skis did for William what the long-gone record player and toy train could not.

Just as you give your child nutritious food and make your child wear warm clothing ultimately for his benefit, so, too, choose gifts wisely for your child. Provide what is most beneficial, not necessarily what is desired. Give gifts that are challenging, bring out your child's talents, and broaden your child's creativity and horizons. Such gifts last far beyond one season!

Who's Who:

Jacob

Genesis 37 and following chapters tell the story of Joseph, the son of Jacob—of multi-colored coat fame. Jacob had eleven sons, but he favored Joseph above all of them. Not only that, but Jacob made no effort to hide his adoration for his then-youngest son. (Later on, he had another son named Benjamin.)

As the famous story goes, Jacob gave Joseph what was for that time an ostentatious gift. According to the Bible, Jacob made Joseph a richly ornamented robe. Not only did he give a gift expressly to Joseph (and not his other sons), but he actually fashioned the robe himself.

This gift, and subsequent events, led his brothers to despise Joseph, and eventually their hatred turned to murder. They considered killing their younger brother, but then decided to sell him as a slave to a caravan of Ishmaelites traveling to Egypt. In the end, God brought good out of this seemingly tragic situation. Still, Jacob suffered years of grief over the loss of his son—and no doubt some of the brothers, especially the oldest, Reuben, felt guilt over this incident.

In giving gifts to children, it is critical not to show partiality. No good can come of it for the recipient or the other children in your family. Choose wisely and fairly.

TALKING THE TALK

THE NAME ALBERT Einstein is synonymous with that of "genius." Many don't know, however, that Einstein was a late talker. His parents grew quite worried about this. Then, at supper one night, he broke his silence with a full sentence, saying, "The soup is too hot." Overjoyed, his greatly relieved parents asked him why he hadn't spoken before. He said, "Because up to now everything was in order."

The difference in parents trying to get their babies and teens to talk is one of language. Babies are learning the parents' language. But parents end up trying to learn the language of their teens! This shift has several stages. First, a parent goes through the "Why?" stage. When parents don't have answers, the child enters his own "I know" stage. Next, he adds vocabulary words he doesn't learn from his parents. "Jam" and "cool" take on new meanings. A child then asks more questions using these words that parents can't answer, such as "Why are you jammin' fifty in a school zone?" and "Is it ever cool to break the law?" Finding that parents still don't have answers, teens take to the telephone to talk to someone who does—another teen.

The solution to the communication gap may very well be: make up some answers!

> **He will fill** your mouth with laughter and your lips with shouts of joy.
> JOB 8:21

Parents of teens and parents of babies have something in common. They spend a great deal of time trying to get their kids to talk.

PAUL SWETS

new insights into ageless questions

My teenager has started rebelling, and I never realized it could be so painful for me as a parent. Why do kids do this, and what can I do about it?

The teen years can be much more tumultuous than the "terrible twos." What makes them more frightening is that a teenager has a much greater opportunity for disaster. They cross streets without holding our hands. They leave the safety of our homes, often behind the wheel of a car. They are capable of having relationships we aren't aware of. And most of all, they are vulnerable (by virtue of sheer proximity) to a vast array of dangers and deception.

At the same time, a teenager is piecing together a new identity—one that is appropriate for the world at large, apart from family. Teens are growing, changing all very quickly. No wonder they are testy at times.

It's a pretty tough period. What's a parent to do?

That's a big question with no simple answer. But here are some suggestions to help you set a firm foundation: 1) Pray continually. God is your first and best and sometimes only defense. 2) Love them. And don't be afraid to show it—often. Nag your teen to death with shows of affection (big hugs) and encouraging words (simple and direct). Ignore the protests. 3) Be tolerant. Tolerate their friends, their moods, their erratic behavior, their confusion, their "teenness." Be tolerant of the small stuff so when you must respond to the big issues, your voice will be heard.

HOW Do YOU MEASURE Up?

How willing are you to examine yourself before looking to point out fault in others?

1. When I take note of the ongoing mental tape of my thoughts, they are:
   A. Focused on finding fault with those around me.
   B. Focused on how my life could be better if only _____ would do _____.
   C. Focused on what I can do to make myself and my life the best it can be.

2. When I think about the circumstances of my life, do I spend time:
   A. Pining over what could have been?
   B. Feeling bitter that my husband didn't take that job in Toledo (or didn't do something years or months ago)?
   C. Focusing on the future and moving forward, placing my trust in God?

3. As I approach each day, I:
   A. Have a strict agenda that allows for little flex.
   B. Think, "Why bother? I can't control anything in my life anyway."
   C. Think about what the people in my life might need, what I must accomplish, and set out to do what I can, allowing for what God may bring into my life.

If you answered "C" to each question, you are probably striking a healthy balance between self-examination and determination. If "B," it's probably time to take some accountability for your life and stop playing the blame game. If you answered "A," pull yourself out of the past and open your eyes and heart to the people around you.

No short quiz can address the complexities of life and relationships, but it can help you begin to examine your thoughts, motives, and actions. God is ready to reveal them to you and help you become more like Christ—the best you can be for yourself and for those around you.

VALUE OF LOOKING INWARD

> IF THERE IS ANYTHING
> WE WISH TO CHANGE
> IN THE CHILD, WE
> SHOULD FIRST EXAMINE
> IT AND SEE WHETHER IT
> IS NOT SOMETHING
> THAT COULD BE BETTER
> CHANGED IN OURSELVES.
>
> C.G. JUNG

Coming down the main walk from the capitol in Washington, D.C., toward Pennsylvania Avenue, one encounters a group of steps. In watching the crowds go up and down those steps, a man once observed that people were continually stumbling on them, while they didn't seem to stumble on any other flights of stairs in the city.

He called the attention of the capitol architect to the matter. The architect couldn't believe this was so until he observed the people for himself. He was amazed at the number of people who stumbled in going up the steps. "I cannot account for it," he said. "I spent weeks in arranging those steps. I had wooden models of them put down at my own place, and I walked over them day after day until I felt sure they were perfect."

A person hearing him speak asked, "Isn't one of your legs shorter than the other, Mr. Olmstead?" Sure enough, the architect had designed the steps of the capitol based on his own inequality of limbs, and had thus made the stairs truly suitable only for those with a similar condition!

First take the beam out of your own eye,
and then you will see clearly to take out the
speck that is in your brother's eye.

LUKE 6:42 AMP

FLYING LESSONS

> ## CHILDREN ARE THE HANDS BY WHICH WE TAKE HOLD OF HEAVEN.
>
> HENRY WARD BEECHER

HENRY WARD Beecher, considered by many to be one of the most effective and powerful pulpit orators in the history of the United States, not only had a reputation for having an extremely sensitive heart, but also for having a great love of the sea. Many of his sermons were laced with loving anecdotes that had seafaring flavor.

Not only did Beecher make the statement at the top of the page, but he had this to say about a mother's relationship with her child:

A babe is a mother's anchor. She cannot swing far from her moorings. And yet a true mother never lives so little in the present as when by the side of the cradle. Her thoughts follow the imagined future of her child. That babe is the boldest of pilots, and guides her fearless thoughts down through scenes of coming years. The old ark never made such voyages as the cradle daily makes.

What a wonderful image to think of a child as being on a voyage from Heaven, through life, to return to Heaven's port one day. What a challenge to think that our children have not come along to join us in our sail through life, but rather, we to join in their voyage!

Jesus said, "Verily I say unto you, whosoever shall not receive the kingdom of God as a little child shall in no wise enter therein."

LUKE 18:17 KJV

TOP **10** TIPS
for Giving Your Children Wings (and teaching them to navigate safely)

1. PRAY FOR YOUR CHILD EVERY DAY—FOR SAFETY, FOR WISDOM, FOR THEIR HEARTS AND SOULS.

2. GIVE YOUR CHILDREN FREEDOM WITHIN THE BOUNDARIES THEY CAN HANDLE.

3. GIVE YOUR FEAR AND ANXIETY ABOUT YOUR CHILD'S SAFETY AND WELL-BEING OVER TO GOD.

4. ENCOURAGE YOUR CHILDREN TO BE A PART OF SITUATIONS WHERE YOU KNOW THEY'LL FIND SUCCESS.

5. CHALLENGE YOUR KIDS TO TEST THEIR LIMITS IN WAYS THAT BUILD CONFIDENCE.

6. RECOGNIZE AND REWARD YOUR CHILDREN'S ACCOMPLISHMENTS, BUT BE CERTAIN THAT THEY KNOW YOUR LOVE IS NOT BASED ON WHAT THEY DO, BUT WHO THEY ARE.

7. TEACH YOUR CHILDREN TO TRUST GOD WITH THEIR LIVES AND THEIR FUTURES.

8. INTRODUCE YOUR CHILDREN TO NEW CULTURES, LANGUAGES, FOODS, MUSIC, BOOKS, ART.

9. DON'T OVER-SCHEDULE YOUR CHILD SO HE HAS NO FREE TIME TO BE CREATIVE OR EXPLORE HIS WORLD INDEPENDENTLY.

10. GIVE YOUR CHILD THE SPACE AND FREEDOM TO FLY AND ENTRUST HIM TO GOD.

CONSIDER THIS!

Believers in Christ have been given personal access to the eternal God, the Alpha and Omega, who is and was and will forever be. He is all-knowing, understanding, and powerful. The man or woman you most esteem here on earth cannot even begin to compare in depth of wisdom or position. God loves you more than you are loved by anyone—more than you love your own child.

What's more, this God desires to be in a personal relationship with you, wants you to call him Father and Lord, wants you to experience His Spirit and His renewal in your life. His compassion never wavers or wanes. And God wants all of this for your children too.

Pray for your children constantly, with hope, honesty, and expectation. You are not alone in your parenting, thanks be to God.

MOTHERS WHO PRAY

Abraham Lincoln is not the only president who has paid tribute to his mother's faith. President Reagan was also reverential about his mother, calling her "one of the kindliest persons I've ever known."

After an assassination attempt on President Reagan's life in March, 1981, he spoke of his mother in a letter: "I found myself remembering that my mother's strongest belief was that all things happen for a reason. She would say we may not understand the why of such things, but if we accept them and go forward, we find, down the road a ways, there was a reason and that everything happens for

> I REMEMBER MY MOTHER'S PRAYERS, AND THEY HAVE ALWAYS FOLLOWED ME. THEY HAVE CLUNG TO ME ALL MY LIFE.
>
> ABRAHAM LINCOLN

the best. Her greatest gift to me was an abiding and unshakable faith in God."

There are many things that a child doesn't remember. He rarely remembers every scraped knee, every reprimand, every home-cooked meal. What a child tends to remember are character traits of a parent, and the way they manifested themselves in a pattern of consistency. Make prayer a daily habit—and let your child overhear you praying for them on a daily basis. They may not remember each and every prayer, but they will remember you as a praying person! And that example will never depart from them.

I prayed for this child, and the Lord
has granted me what I asked of him.

1 SAMUEL 1:27

DESIGNED
WITH PURPOSE

Henry Kendall from Boston and Richard Taylor from Medicine Hat, Canada, achieved a breakthrough in man's understanding of matter and furthered the theory of the structure of protons and neutrons.

Mikhail Gorbachev from Privolnoye, USSR, contributed to a breakthrough in man's understanding about how East and West might better relate through "glasnost," a policy of open political coexistence.

Octavio Paz from Mexico City was a political commentator, diplomat, essayist, and poet who wrote passionately throughout his life about man's needs for "wider horizons."

> BABIES ARE SUCH A NICE WAY TO START PEOPLE.
>
> DON HEROLD

Edward Donnall Thomas from Mart, Texas, proved that it was possible to transplant organs to save the lives of dying patients.

Harry M. Markowitz from Chicago, developed the theory that combinations of economic assets of differing risks could decrease the overall risk of investment.

What did these six men have in common? Two things. First, although they represented vastly diverse heritages, interests, and talents, all won Nobel prizes in 1990. And second, nobody could have predicted their success before they were born.

EVE CONCEIVED . . . AND SAID,
I HAVE GOTTEN A MAN FROM THE LORD.

GENESIS 4:1 KJV

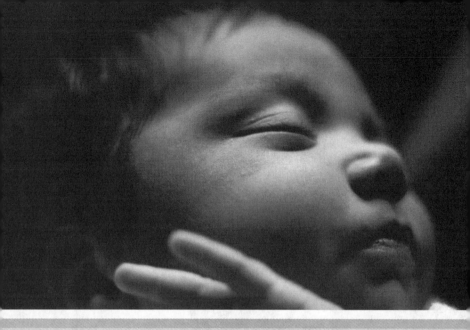

WISE WORDS

You created my inmost being; you knit me together in my mother's womb. I praise you because I am fearfully and wonderfully made; your works are wonderful, I know that full well. My frame was not hidden from you when I was made in the secret place. When I was woven together in the depths of the earth, your eyes saw my unformed body. All the days ordained from me were written in your book before one of them came to be.

PSALM 139:13-16

booklist

- *Growing a Spiritually Strong Family*
  by Dennis and Barbara Rainey

- *Fantastic Families: 6 Proven Steps to
  Building a Strong Family Workbook*
  by Nick Stinnett

- *The Light of Home: Ten Inspiring
  Pictures of a Strong Family*
  by Dr. John Trent

- *Keeping Your Family Strong
  in a World Gone Wrong*
  by Kevin Leman

- *The Home Team*
  by Nate Adams

- *Family First: Your Step-by-Step Plan
  for Creating a Phenomenal Family*
  by Phillip C. McGraw

HOME TEAM

IT WAS A LONG, HARD road that took the Chandler children out of the cotton fields and out of poverty in Mississippi. All nine children have memories of a sharecropper's cabin and nothing to wear and nothing to eat. But today, all nine are college graduates!

Their parents borrowed two dollars to buy a bus ticket for son Cleveland. He worked his way through school and became chairman of the economics department at Howard University. Luther went to the University of Omaha and became the Public Service Employment Manager for Kansas City. He helped brother James get to Omaha, and then to Yale for graduate work. James, in turn, helped Herman, who is now a technical manager in Dallas. Donald works in Minneapolis.

The children also helped themselves—picking cotton, pulling corn, stripping millet, digging potatoes. Fortson went to Morehouse and is a Baptist minister in Colorado. Princess has an M.A. from Indiana and is a schoolteacher. Gloria is also a teacher. Bessie has an M.A. and is the dietitian at a veterans' hospital.

Together, the children bought a house for their parents in 1984. Nine players make a baseball team, but nine Chandler children have made an unbeatable team for the game of life!

> **Making children a part** of a family team is of critical importance to the kind of adults that they will become.
>
> DR. WILLIAM MITCHELL AND DR. CHARLES PAUL CONN

How **good** and how **pleasant** it is for **brethren** to **dwell** together in **unity!**

PSALM 133:1 KJV

POSSIBILITIES OF PRAYER

Like many women, Carol found herself routinely emptying her husband's pockets before doing his laundry. She often pulled lists from his pockets, including prayer lists. Her husband rarely listed people's names, only what he was praying that the Lord would do in their lives.

> **Daily** prayers will diminish your cares.
> BETTY MILLS

One Monday a woman named Betty, a delivery woman who picked up and delivered her husband's uniforms, came to Carol's door. Carol had never seen Betty smile before, but this day, she glowed. She said, "I want to thank you for the prayers." Then she explained, "Every week I clean out the cargo pockets of your husband's fatigues. I thought that God had given up on me, but He has been speaking to me through the prayers that I find in your husband's pockets. I was starving for God and for His Word. Those scraps of paper with prayers were like food. I couldn't wait until Monday to see if I would find another message. I claimed each one as my own. Yesterday I accepted Jesus as my Savior. My new church has a group who ministers to new believers."

Only God knows the final outcome of all your prayer requests. He alone is the "Finisher" and the great "Amen" of what you request before His throne.

Evening, and morning, and at noon, will I pray, and cry aloud: and he shall hear my voice.

PSALM 55:17 KJV

✓ JUST DO IT

Make a list of people in your life who could use your prayers, perhaps people you wouldn't think to pray for on a regular basis. It may be:

- Your child's principal or music teacher.
- A school bus driver.
- Your child's classmate.

The following is a prayer you can use to pray for the people on your list:

Lord, I'm not certain where these people stand in their relationship with You, but I pray that You would draw them to You. Please work in their lives this day. Amen.

You may never realize how God has worked in their lives or see amazing outward answers to your prayers. But you can be certain that no prayer is ever offered for another in vain.

LIVIN' BEHIND THE WHEEL

A MOTHER ONCE FACED the prospect of sixteen trips to church! Various combinations of her children were serving in various roles for three different Sunday services. The one serving the seven o'clock service had to be there fifteen minutes early to robe and light the candles. So Mom doubled back for the kids who were going to attend that service since they weren't ready when she left the first time. And so it went for each service—two trips—and the same coming home.

In all, three services, Sunday school, and two different youth group meetings, and the total number of trips was sixteen! Since the church was six miles from their home, she drove ninety-six miles that morning, all before lunch. She moaned to herself more than once, "This is the last time my husband goes out of town on business over a weekend!"

To her dismay, she found a police-car in their driveway upon her final trip home. An officer had been sent to check on a fairly large number of past-due parking tickets acquired by her husband. "Been busy this morning?" the officer asked. The woman recounted the litany of her morning. And then the officer asked the worst possible question, "May I see your license?" It had been expired for two months!

lighten up

What do you think about while you're waiting to pick up your kids? Snack on this food for thought:

- If at first you don't succeed, skydiving is not for you.
- Vital papers will demonstrate their vitality by moving from where you left them to where you can't find them.
- The trouble with doing something right the first time is that nobody appreciates how difficult it was.
- It may be that your sole purpose in life is simply to serve as a warning to others.
- Ray's Law: You can't fall off the floor.
- Eagles may soar, but weasels aren't sucked into jet engines.
- Experience is something you don't get until just after you need it.
- The sooner you fall behind, the more time you'll have to catch up.
- A clear conscience is usually the sign of a bad memory.
- Borrow money from pessimists—they don't expect it back.

In Your presence is

A suburban mother's role is to **deliver** children obstetrically once, and **by car** forever after.

fulness of joy. PSALM 16:11 AMP

Fun Trivia

A mother's love is so strong and resilient that we have dedicated a day to celebrate it. How much do you know about Mother's Day?

Why is Mother's Day celebrated on the second Sunday in May?

Mother's Day was officially proclaimed in what state?
What incident may have provided the inspiration for Mother's Day?

Anna Jarvis, the person credited with initiating the first Mother's Day celebration at Andrews Church, chose the date because she lost her own mother on the second Sunday of May.

In 1908, two years after the first celebration at Andrews Church, Governor William E. Glasscock of West Virginia officially proclaimed the first Mother's Day.

It is believed that Anna Jarvis was inspired by her mother's efforts shortly after the Civil War. Anna's mother organized the Union and Confederate mothers of her little community in an effort to bring their sons together again in forgiveness and friendship.

ENDURING LOVE

A **mother's** love is **patient** and **forgiving**
when all others are forsaking,
and it **never fails** or falters, even though
the **heart** is **breaking.** HELEN STEINER RICE

An angel strolled out of heaven one beautiful day and winged its way to earth. On a quest for beauty, he wandered through both fields and cities beholding the glories of nature and the finest works of art. As sunset approached, he thought, *What keepsake can I take back to show my heavenly friends the beauty of earth?*

He noticed a patch of beautiful and fragrant wildflowers in the field where he was standing, and he decided to pluck them to make a bouquet. Then, passing a home, he saw through the open door a baby smiling from its crib. He took the smile with him, too. At another home,

he saw through an open window a mother pouring out her love to her precious child as she stooped to kiss him "Goodnight." The angel decided to take the mother's love, too.

As the angel flew homeward through the pearly gates, he noticed to his astonishment that the flowers in his hand had withered. The baby's smile had changed into a frown. Only the mother's love remained as he had found it. He said to those who greeted him, "Here is the only thing I found today on earth that could retain its beauty and goodness all the way to Heaven—the sweetness of a mother's love!"

Love is patient, love is kind.
It does not envy, it does
not boast, it is not proud. . . .
Love never fails.

1 CORINTHIANS 13:4,8

NEVER SATISFIED

> **ASK** YOUR **CHILD** WHAT HE **WANTS** FOR DINNER ONLY IF HE'S **BUYING.**
>
> FRAN LEBOWITZ

EVERY morning a mother announced, "This is not a restaurant; there are no menus." She still got orders as she packed school lunches for all her children.

"Peanut butter and jelly?" one would cry.

"Oh no! Why can't we ever have cheese." That child seemed to have totally forgotten that yesterday's sandwich was cheese and he had complained it wasn't peanut butter.

"Grape jelly?" another asked. "Can't we ever get strawberry?"

Yet another would say, "Leave the jelly off mine, but can I have two sandwiches?"

Over the years, the mother felt confident that she had finally learned what each child liked.

Her youngest, Jim, always seemed to return home with an empty sack, a fact she took as a high compliment. Until one day when she handed Jim his sack and said, "Enjoy your lunch."

He replied, "Oh, I'm not gonna eat this, Mom. I'm trading with Josh. His Mom bakes cookies, and he told me he'd trade lunches today if I let him play with my football. Isn't that great? I can hardly wait!"

"Does anybody ever want to trade for your lunch?" the mother asked hopefully.

"Naw," the boy replied. "But don't worry about me. I still eat well. Nobody else in my class has a football."

If they obey and serve Him, they shall spend their days in prosperity . . . and joy.

JOB 36:11 AMP

TOP **10** TIPS for Getting Good Food into Your Kids

So much of mothering has to do with feeding your kids. So much has come out recently directly linking good nutrition in the early years (even during pregnancy) and quality of health later in life. Here are a few general tips to help you manage the food situation (in some cases, war) in your home:

1. INTRODUCE VEGGIES BEFORE FRUITS WHEN STARTING YOUR CHILD ON SOLID FOOD.

2. SERVE YOUR CHILDREN HEALTHY SNACKS.

3. KEEP MORE HEALTHY SNACKS IN THE CAR.

4. INTRODUCE YOUR KIDS TO ALL TYPES OF FOOD.

5. KNOW THE DIFFERENT STAGES OF DEVELOPMENTAL EATING PATTERNS —TODDLERS MIGHT QUIT EATING MUCH FOR A COUPLE DAYS AND THEN EAT LIKE A HORSE.

6. SET A GOOD EXAMPLE BY EATING HEALTHILY YOURSELF.

7. GIVE YOUR KIDS VITAMIN SUPPLEMENTS.

8. INTRODUCE YOUR KIDS TO THE JOYS OF DRINKING WATER, AND SKIP THE SODA.

9. TEACH YOUR CHILDREN THAT GOD WANTS THEM TO TAKE CARE OF THEIR BODIES.

10. INSTILL IN YOUR CHILDREN A HEALTHY VIEW OF FOOD.

CONSIDER THIS!

As a parent, you have the privilege of watching your child experience sights, smells, sounds, and tastes for the very first time. Why not dispense with your adult lenses and agendas, and experience the wonder of all of this newness with your child? Every age and stage presents a new opportunity for a mom to see things in fresh ways, through the eyes of her child.

The Romantic poet William Wordsworth captured one such moment beautifully with the following:

> I have seen
> A curious child, who dwelt upon a tract
> Of inland ground, applying to his ear
> The convolutions of a smooth-lipped shell,
> To which, in silence hushed, his very soul
> Listened intensely; and his countenance soon
> Brightened with joy, for from within were heard
> Murmurings, whereby the monitor expressed
> Mysterious union with its native sea.

ALTERED PERSPECTIVE

In 1981, Elizabeth Glaser gave birth to a girl, Ariel. But moments after Ari was born, she began to hemorrhage. Elizabeth remembers watching silently as Ari received a transfusion of seven pints of blood—blood contaminated by HIV. Four years later, Ariel began to suffer baffling stomach pains and draining fatigue. She underwent a battery of tests, one of which gave a name to her illness: AIDS.

After Ariel's death, Elizabeth became a leading AIDS activist, cofounding the Pediatric AIDS Foundation. Many consider her to be the most effective AIDS lobbyist in the nation. She says of Ariel, "It was Ari who taught me to love when all I wanted to do was hate. She taught me to be brave when all I felt was fear. And she taught me to help others when all I wanted to do was help myself. I am active in fighting AIDS because I want to be a person she would be proud of; I was so proud of her. . . . I think about her courage and I am able to go on."

About living with HIV, Elizabeth said, "Everything—from making peanut butter sandwiches and watching Jake [her son] play ball to planting the garden—has significance to me."

Children add another dimension to our lives—one that focuses on someone else besides ourselves.

> GOD SENDS CHILDREN FOR ANOTHER PURPOSE THAN MERELY TO KEEP UP THE RACE—TO ENLARGE OUR HEARTS, TO MAKE US UNSELFISH, AND FULL OF KINDLY SYMPATHIES AND AFFECTIONS.
>
> MARY HOWITT

My little children, let us not love in word, neither in tongue; but in deed and in truth.

1 JOHN 3:18 KJV

LEARN AND LIVE

If a child lives with criticism
He learns to condemn;
If a child lives with hostility
He learns to fight;
If a child lives with ridicule
He learns to be shy;
If a child lives with shame
He learns to feel guilty.
BUT
If a child lives with tolerance
He learns to be patient;
If a child lives with encouragement
He learns confidence;
If a child lives with praise
He learns to appreciate;
If a child lives with fairness
He learns justice;
If a child lives with security
He learns to have faith;
If a child lives with approval
He learns to like himself;
If a child lives with acceptance and friendship
He learns to find LOVE in the world!
—Dorothy Lawe Holt

> **Beloved** follow not that which is evil, but that which is good.
> 3 JOHN 11 KJV

CHILDREN ARE NATURAL MIMICS—
THEY ACT LIKE THEIR PARENTS IN SPITE OF EVERY
ATTEMPT TO TEACH THEM GOOD MANNERS.

WISE WORDS

I urge you to live a life worthy of the
calling you have received. Be completely
humble and gentle; be patient, bearing
with one another in love. Make every
effort to keep the unity of the Spirit
through the bond of peace. There is one
body and one Spirit—just as you were
called to one hope when you were
called—one Lord, one faith, one baptism;
one God and Father of all, who is over all
and through all and in all. But to each
one of us grace has been given as Christ
apportioned it.

EPHESIANS 4:1-7

booklist

read more about it...potential

- *Keys to Developing Your Child's Self-Esteem*
  by Carl E. Pritchardt, Ph.D.

- *The Confident Child: Raising Children
  to Believe in Themselves*
  by Terri Apter

- *365 Ways to Build Your Child's Self-Esteem*
  by Cheri Fuller

- *10-Minute Life Lessons for Kids: 52 Fun and
  Simple Games and Activities to Teach Your
  Child Honesty, Trust, Love, and Other
  Important Values*
  by Jamie C. Miller

- *Building Self-Esteem in Children*
  by Patricia H. Berne; Louis M. Savary

LOOKING FORWARD

SHORTLY AFTER ARRIVING in the major leagues, pitcher Orel Hershiser was called to the office of Dodgers General Manager Tommy Lasorda. Orel knew the news wasn't going to be good. He had had a disappointing start as a relief pitcher. Lasorda, however, didn't focus on his record. He said instead, "You don't believe in yourself! You're scared to pitch in the big leagues!

"Who do you think these hitters are, Babe Ruth? Ruth's dead! You've got good stuff. If you didn't, I wouldn't have brought you up. I've seen guys come and go, son, and you've got it! You gotta go out there and do it on the mound. Be a bulldog out there. That's gonna be your new name: Bulldog. Bulldog Hershiser. I want you, starting today, to believe you are the best pitcher in baseball. I want you to look at that hitter and say, 'There's no way you can ever hit me.'"

Hershiser writes in his autobiography, *Out of the Blue,* "I couldn't get over that Tommy Lasorda felt I was worth this much time and effort. . . . He believed I had more potential. He believed I had big league stuff." The next game, Hershiser pitched for three innings, and gave up only one hit.

Talk more to your child about their potential than their track record. They have more potential than history!

> **[Love] bears all** things, believes all things, hopes all things, endures all things.
>
> 1 CORINTHIANS 13:7 NRSV

My mother said to me, "If you become a soldier you'll be a general; if you become a monk you'll end up as the pope." Instead, I became a painter and wound up as Picasso.

PABLO PICASSO

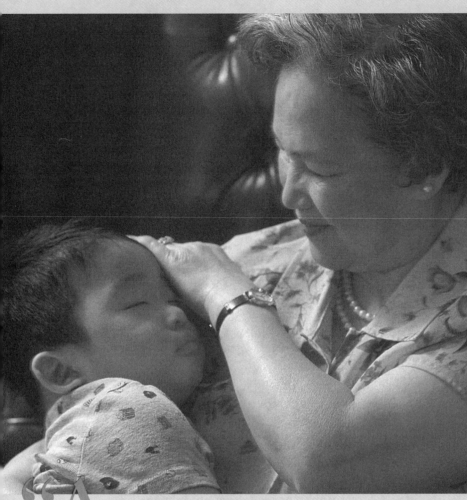

"A good deed is never lost; he who sows **COURTESY** reaps friendship, and he who plants **kindness** gathers love."

Saint Basil

A DEED THAT LIVES ON

In the late nineteenth century, a member of Parliament traveled to Scotland to make a speech. He traveled to Edinburgh by train, and then took a carriage southward to his destination. The carriage, however, became mired in mud. A Scottish farm boy came to the rescue with a team of horses and pulled the carriage loose. The politician asked the boy how much he owed him. "Nothing," the lad replied. "Are you sure?" the politician pressed, but the boy declined payment. "Well, is there anything I can do for you? What do you want to be when you grow up?" The boy responded, "A doctor." The aristocratic Englishman offered to help the young Scot go to the university, and he followed through on his pledge.

More than half a century later, Winston Churchill lay dangerously ill with pneumonia—stricken while attending a wartime conference in Morocco. A new "wonder drug" was administered to him, a drug called penicillin that had been discovered by Sir Alexander Fleming. Fleming was the young Scottish lad once befriended. His benefactor? Randolph Churchill, Winston's father!

Sometimes the good that you do may very well come back to you in the form of the miracle you need.

Who's Who:

Lois & Eunice

The apostle Paul begins his second letter to Timothy with a greeting that includes these words: "I have been reminded of your sincere faith, which first lived in your grandmother Lois and in your mother Eunice and, I am persuaded, now lives in you also" (2 Timothy 1:5).

Not much is known about Grandma Lois or Mother Eunice except that they bestowed a legacy of faith on their children and grandchildren. Eunice, we can assume, also taught Timothy the Scriptures and began to cultivate faith in him when he was very young (2 Timothy 3:15). Timothy became Paul's assistant and worked with him in the cause of spreading Christ's message.

Mothers are known for showing care and compassion to their children, but there is no greater deed and no more satisfying return than introducing your child to faith in Christ. When Lois modeled and taught her daughter Eunice about God, she probably had no idea how many she would influence through her grandson and the letters that were written to him. So important was the contribution of this mother and grandmother that it was deemed worthy of sacred biblical text.

SEEING IS DOING

LITTLE DANNY, ONLY SIX months old, was bitten on the hand by a rat as he lay in his crib. His screams awakened everyone in the house. His parents rushed him to the hospital and the doctors did all they could do with the limited medical techniques available at the time, but the poor baby was just about given up for dead. His mother fell to her knees and screamed aloud, "Please, God, spare him, and I will vow to You that I will beg pennies from door to door for a whole year to give to the poor. Spare my baby. Please, God, spare my baby." His father, too, dropped to his knees, prayed, and vowed that he would never gamble again.

> **He who** walks with the wise grows wise.
> PROVERBS 13:20

Miraculously, Danny lived, perhaps even with rabies from the rat. And for an entire year, his mother took the streetcar to the end of the line, and walked all the way back downtown, begging pennies from door to door. Sometimes, doors were slammed in her face, but she persevered for a full year, pleading in her Middle Eastern accent, "Blease give bennies to the boor. I bromise God." His father never again gambled.

The memory is the chief reason Danny Thomas cites for keeping his vow to St. Jude and for his generous fundraising on behalf of the St. Jude Children's Research Hospital in Memphis, Tennessee.

Any child will learn to worship God who lives his daily life with adults who worship Him.

ANNA B. MOW

new insights into ageless questions

All my life I've heard people say we are to give our lives to God, but I'm worried. What if I do that and then regret it? Am I saying by such a commitment that I will do whatever God asks me to do—even if it means doing something completely out of character for me or something drastic like leaving my family or moving to a foreign country? What if I make a vow to God and then my husband doesn't approve of what God tells me?

Whoa! You are getting way ahead of yourself. First of all, God would not ask you to do something entirely against your natural inclinations. The gifts, talents, and motivations that drive you each day were given to you by Him—and for His purposes in your life. What He will ask you to do is develop the gifts you have and use them for His glory—that might be in your home, in your church, in your community, or even in a foreign country.

You can also be sure that God will not ask you to do something that causes a breach in your marriage or jeopardize the safety of your children. That isn't to say that your husband will accept and approve of everything the first time he hears about it. But you can pray if you feel strongly about something. When you do, God has a way of bringing husbands around to His way of thinking. If your husband stands his ground, God would expect you to stay put, honor your husband, and put your trust in Him.

Committing your life to God is more than an instance in time; it's a process. All God asks is that you open your heart and mind to His gentle urgings and desire in your heart to become all He has called you to be.

DOUBLY BUSY

LILLIAN TOOK AN ACTIVE role in Sunday school work. She didn't teach a class, but she served on a number of committees. Once she called on a woman who had just moved to town to ask her to serve on a fund-raising committee. "I'd be glad to if I had the time," the woman said, "but I have three young sons and they keep me on the run. I'm sure if you have a boy of your own, you'll understand how much trouble three can be."

Lillian replied, "Of course, that's quite all right. And I do understand."

"Have you any children, Mrs. Gilbreth?" the woman asked. Lillian replied, "Oh, yes."

The woman pursued the line, "Any boys?"

Lillian said, "Yes, indeed."

The woman persisted, "May I ask how many?"

Lillian graciously replied, "Certainly. I have six boys."

The woman gulped, "Six boys? Imagine a family of six!"

Lillian added, "Oh, there are more in the family than that. I have six girls, too."

As Frank B. Gilbreth Jr. and Ernestine Gilbreth Carey tell in their book *Cheaper by the Dozen,* the newcomer then whispered, "I surrender. When is the next meeting of the committee? I'll be there, Mrs. Gilbreth. I'll be there."

lighten up

Mixed Messages

• Why do we order cheeseburgers and large fries and wash it down with a diet soda?

• Why do drugstores make the sick walk all the way to the back of the store to get their medications while healthy people can buy cigarettes at the front?

• Why do banks leave both doors open and then chain the pens to the counters?

• Why do we leave cars worth thousands of dollars in the driveway and put our useless junk in the garage?

• Why do we expect moms who stay at home with their children—regardless of the number—to answer "no" when asked, "Do you work?" Duh!

> "Any mother could perform the jobs of several air-traffic controllers with ease."
>
> LISA ALTHER

does not eat the bread of idleness. PROVERBS 31:27 NRSV

NEVER TOO SERIOUS

> **MAN** HAS HIS **WILL**—BUT **WOMAN** HAS HER **WAY.**
>
> OLIVER WENDELL HOLMES

A MAN LISTENED with great admiration to a well-known and very popular leader make a speech at a banquet. He not only hung on every word the speaker said, but studied his appearance. He felt honored to be seated next to the speaker's wife, and he candidly told her that her husband was one of his heroes.

During the speech, the man noticed that the speaker had monogrammed socks. Intrigued by this, he looked closer and saw that the monogram had four letters, rather than the usual two or three initials. Furthermore, the letters didn't seem to have any relationship to the man's name—they were "TGIF."

After the speech was over and the man had complimented the speaker, he turned to the wife and said, "I couldn't help but notice the monogram on your husband's socks. Is there some reason he has chosen 'Thank Goodness It's Friday' for a monogram?" She shook her head and said, "Oh, that's not what the letters mean. The monograms are there to help him get dressed. They stand for 'Toes Go In First!'"

Let those also who love Your name be joyful in You and be in high spirits.

PSALM 5:11 AMP

TOP **10** TIPS for Bringing Levity into Life

Sometimes life isn't funny or light. But you and your kids need to build in time for letting loose, enjoying life, and sharing some good laughs.

1. SURPRISE YOUR FAMILY WITH A NIGHT OF WATCHING FUNNY FLICKS.

2. WHEN POSSIBLE, DIFFUSE ARGUMENTS WITH YOUR KIDS BY BRINGING HUMOR INTO IT.

3. TAKE NOTICE OF THE HUMOROUS THINGS YOUR CHILDREN DO AND SAY.

4. LISTEN TO YOUR KIDS' JOKES (EVEN THE DREADED "KNOCK-KNOCK" SERIES), AND GIVE THEM A LAUGH.

5. PICK A FUNNY, FAMILY-FRIENDLY SHOW ON TV, AND WATCH IT TOGETHER WEEKLY.

6. SHOW YOUR KIDS THAT MANY SITUATIONS IN LIFE HAVE THE SILVER LINING OF HUMOR.

7. LAUGH WITH YOUR FAMILY, A LOT.

8. LET YOUR KIDS POKE FUN AT YOU, THEMSELVES, AND EACH OTHER IN HEALTHY DOSES AND WAYS.

9. KNOW THAT HUMOR IS A GIFT FROM GOD.

10. WITH THAT IN MIND, LIGHTEN UP EVERY CHANCE YOU GET!

CONSIDER THIS!

You may have a great relationship with your parents and your parents-in-law—or maybe not. But one thing you can be sure of, your children are watching your every move, and they are picking up clues about how parents should be treated. You don't have to be untruthful, but it is important that your kids see you showing respect for your parents or parents-in-law.

Proverbs 23:22 says, "Listen to your father, who gave you life, and do not despise your mother when she is old." It is a scripture you should read often and a principle you should live out in your actions. When your children see how you speak about and treat your own parents, they will store that away for a future time.

ALL EYES ON YOU

According to an old legend, there once was a man who had an only son, to whom he gave everything he owned. When his son grew up, he was unkind to his father, refused to support him, and turned him out of his own house.

OUR CHILDREN ARE WATCHING US LIVE, AND WHAT WE ARE SHOUTS LOUDER THAN ANYTHING WE CAN SAY.

WILFERD A. PETERSON

As the old man prepared to leave his home, he turned to his young grandson and said, "Go and fetch the covering from my bed, that I may go and sit by the wayside and wrap myself in it and beg for alms."

The child burst into tears and ran for the covering. But rather than take it to his grandfather, he ran to his father and said, "Oh father, grandfather has asked for this so he can keep himself warm as he sits by the road and begs. Please cut it into two pieces. Half of it will be large enough for grandfather. And you may want the other half when I am grown to be a man and turn you out-of-doors."

The child's words struck to the very core of the uncaring son and he ran to his father, asked his forgiveness, and took care of him until his death.

What we do always comes across to our children as the loudest and clearest of messages.

In everything set them an example by doing what is good.

TITUS 2:7

HEAVEN IN A SMILE

A pastor tells the story of how, during the twelve years of his pastorate at one particular church, he had a custom during the Sunday morning service of calling the children forward just before his sermon so that they could go to a special "children's church" and hear a sermon geared especially for them. During their processional to the assembly hall, the children marched past the pulpit, and the pastor made it a point to smile at each child. In return, he received their smiles. "It was one of the high points of the service," he recalled.

One day, however, the pastor apparently missed smiling at one child. A curly-headed four-year-old ran out of the procession and threw herself into the arms of her mother, sobbing as if her heart was broken.

After the service the pastor sought out the mother to find out what had happened. The mother explained that after her child had quieted, she asked what caused the tears. The child had said, "I smiled at God, but He didn't smile back at me!" The pastor reflected, "To that child, I stood for God. I had failed with my smile, and the world went dark."

Smile at each person you meet today. You may never know how much you have brightened a life!

> A HAPPY HEART MAKES THE FACE CHEERFUL.
>
> PROVERBS 15:13

WHAT SUNSHINE IS TO FLOWERS, SMILES ARE TO HUMANITY. THEY ARE BUT TRIFLES, TO BE SURE BUT, SCATTERED ALONG LIFE'S PATHWAY, THE GOOD THEY DO IS INCONCEIVABLE.

JOSEPH ADDISON

WISE WORDS

My soul, there is a country
Far beyond the stars
Where stands a winged sentry
All skillful in the wars:
There, above noise and danger,
Sweet Peace is crown'd with smiles,
And One born in a manger
Commands the beauteous files.

HENRY VAUGHAN

A smile brings a bit of heaven's light to earth.

booklist

read more about it...staying positive

- **365 Strategies for Positive Single Parenting**
  by Susan Brown

- **Parenting Guide To Positive Discipline**
  by Paula Spencer

- **The Power of Positive Parenting:
  A Wonderful Way to Raise Children**
  by Glenn I. Latham

- **Positive Discipline A-Z, from Toddlers to
  Teens, 1001 Solutions to Everyday Parenting
  Problems**
  by Jane Nelsen, Ed.D.

- **Positive Parenting with a Plan (Grades K-12):
  F.A.M.I.L.Y. Rules**
  by Dr. Matthew A. Johnson

- **Positive Parenting from A to Z**
  by Karen Renshaw Joslin

FOCUS ON THE POSITIVE

A MOTHER ONCE LEFT her children with her single sister in order to work for three weeks overseas. Although she missed her children tremendously, she was also glad for a break. She was feeling worn out as a single parent, struggling to juggle her job and her role as a mother. The demands of constant discipline sometimes seemed too much. As she prepared to return to her family, she thought, *I wonder how Sis coped. I hope she heeded my parting words not to let them get away with murder. The last thing she looked forward to was a round of arguing and reprimanding.*

To her great surprise, she arrived at her sister's home to find her children playing quietly,

Give your troubles to God: He will be up all night anyway.

eager to see her but quick to obey her sister's slightest request. "What did you do?" she whispered to her sister. "They're never this well behaved!" Her sister replied, "Nothing, really. Before you left, I read a little article about parenting, and I just did what it said."

The woman said, "What was it? Give me the formula!"

The sister picked up the article and read, "Tell children what to do, far more than you tell them what not to do. And then praise them for what they do—instead of criticizing them for what they don't do." Smiling at her sister, she added, "It seemed to work!"

Anxiety in the heart of a man weighs it down, but a good word makes it glad.

PROVERBS 12:25 NASB

OPPORTUNITY TO LISTEN

A busy mother of four children found her job as wife and mom a careful balancing act. Each day was filled to the brim with a part-time job, home chores, and chauffeur duty. She had found the most efficient way for her to handle the weekly grocery shopping was to go alone, unhampered by "help" that usually inflated her grocery bill and strained her patience.

On one shopping day, her thirteen-year-old son asked, "Where ya goin', Mom?" She replied, "To the grocery store. I'll be back soon." Her son asked, "Can I go with you?" She almost had the words "some other time" out of her mouth when something inside checked her and she heard herself say, "OK."

> **The more a child** becomes aware of a mother's willingness to listen, the more a mother will begin to hear.

Once in the car, she braced herself for the struggle she anticipated over the use of the radio. Instead, her son began to talk. "When I grow up, I'm going to be rich," he announced. "Oh?" she said.

"Yeah," he said. "Then I can give my kids everything they want." She asked, "Do you know any kid who gets everything he wants?" Her son gave her the name of such a child. "Do you like him?" Mom asked.

After a long pause, he grinned and said, "Naw, he's the meanest, most unhappy kid I know. His dad's never around, and his mom's always too busy."

If you want to know—really know—your child, take time to listen to them.

Let the wise listen and add to their learning, and let the discerning get guidance.

PROVERBS 1:5

to do | urgent

No matter how many children you have, each one deserves to have some one-on-one time alone with you on a regular basis. This won't be easy given a mom's time limitations. Consider these ideas:

- Include your child in an activity you normally do alone—cooking, folding laundry, planting flowers.
- Take your child to lunch or breakfast.
- Get tickets to an event you know your child will love.
- Read a different book with each child.

Pray that God will bless this time and provide opportunity for you to really communicate with your child. Remember, living together doesn't necessarily mean being together. Make time to keep the lines of relationship open.

"When people ask me
WHAT I DO,
I always say I am a
mother first."

JACQUELINE JACKSON

JOB DESCRIPTIONS

Popular writer and speaker Tony Campolo tells a story about his wife. When he was on the faculty of the University of Pennsylvania, his wife was often invited to faculty gatherings, and inevitably a woman lawyer or sociologist would confront her with the question, often framed in a condescending tone of voice, "And what is it that you do, my dear?"

Mrs. Campolo gave this as her response: "I am socializing two Homosapiens in the dominant values of the Judeo-Christian tradition in order that they might be instruments for the transformation of the social order into the teleologically prescribed utopia inherent in the eschaton." Then she would politely and kindly ask the other person, "And what is it that you do?"

The other person's response was rarely as overpowering!

Too often women feel as if they should apologize for being mothers or wives who "work at home" for the betterment of their families and husbands. In reality, these roles can be noble callings—ones with far-reaching impact and eternal consequences!

Who's Who:

Hortense Odlum

Hortense Odlum, a wife and mother of three, was the highly successful president of Bonwit Teller, a women's store in New York City. In fact, she was the first woman to hold such a position. Here's what she had to say about her role as a mother versus her role as a businesswoman: "No satisfactions which I have felt from business (and they have been very great) could have outweighed the satisfactions which came through bearing and rearing my children. I quite honestly would chuck without hesitation every little triumph and success which have come to me through my business career, if having them meant never having had the experiences and joys which were a part of my marriage and motherhood."

It is obvious that Hortense Odlum regarded her work as a mother to be greatly superior to any professional position she might hold—and yet the history books note only her performance outside her home. It says nothing of the legacy of love and nurturing she bestowed on her children.

Whatever roles you take on in your life as a woman, know that there is great and lasting value in your position of wife and mother.

HOW Do YOU MEASURE Up?

Where are your priorities when it comes to making time that is devoted to God? Take this little quiz to get a handle on where your priorities lie.

1. The Bible in my house is:
    A. Picked up and read on a daily basis.
    B. Taken to church only on Sundays.
    C. Collecting dust somewhere.

2. Our family attends a house of worship:
    A. Most Sundays and sometimes for a Bible study during the week.
    B. Sometimes, if we don't have a conflict.
    C. Holidays, if we can get it together.

3. I take time to devote to God:
    A. Nearly every day.
    B. Nearly every week.
    C. Nearly every month (on a Sunday).

4. God is:
    A. At the center of my life.
    B. A part of my life, like exercising and eating right.
    C. Out there somewhere.

If you answered A to most questions, you probably are placing your relationship with God at the center of your life. If B, it may be that you're giving God an equal standing with all the other "important" elements in your life when He should be Lord of All. If C, you may want to unearth your Bible and seek a better understanding of God and what Scripture says about humanity in relation to God. No matter what, it's important to bear in mind that God is a loving, compassionate Father who desires to hear from His children and who wants to do great things in your life.

MAKING TIME FOR GOD

HAPPY IS THE CHILD . . . WHO SEES MOTHER AND FATHER RISING EARLY, OR GOING ASIDE REGULARLY, TO KEEP TIMES WITH THE LORD.

LARRY CHRISTENSON

Parents today often use dozens of excuses to justify not taking their children to church or having a family devotional time, but if that urge strikes you, remember the family of Lydia Murphy. She moved with her parents to Shawnee, Kansas, in 1859, and she writes of their first night in their new home, "The family Bible rested in the center of the room. We gathered around the table, seated on boxes and improvised chairs while the usual evening family prayers were held after the reading of a chapter of the Scriptures. During the fifty years of his Kansas citizenship, this morning and evening scripture reading and prayer was not once omitted in my father's house."

The Murphys had been devout Methodists, but the nearest Methodist church was ten miles away. They therefore secured the services of a circuit-riding Methodist minister and opened their own home for worship, welcoming neighbors of all denominations. Within months, their home had become the center of both the social and religious life of the community. Services were held every two weeks on Saturdays. At other times, neighbors took turns reading Scriptures, leading prayers, and teaching Sunday school!

A child who sees his parents spend time with God has a sense of security that little else can ever establish.

Let the heart of them rejoice that seek the LORD.
Seek the LORD, and his strength: seek his face evermore.

PSALM 105:3-4

FOOD RULES

> A **FOOD** IS **NOT**
> NECESSARILY
> **ESSENTIAL** JUST
> BECAUSE YOUR
> CHILD **HATES** IT.
>
> MOTHER TERESA

IN *FAMILY—THE Ties That Bind and Gag!* Erma Bombeck writes: "In retrospect, it was only a matter of time before the Family Dinner Hour passed into history and fast foods took over. . . . My pot roast gave way to pizza. . . . My burgers couldn't compete with the changing numbers under the Golden Arches. I couldn't even do chicken . . . right!

"The old rules for eating at home—sit up straight, chew your food, and don't laugh with cottage cheese in your mouth—didn't fit the new ambiance. A new set of rules emerged." Bombeck suggests these among the new rules:

When ordering from the backseat of the car, do not cup your mouth over Daddy's ear and shout.

Never order more than you can balance between your knees. Front-of-the-car seating is better than backseat if you have a choice. The dashboard offers space for holding beverages.

Afterward, each person should be responsible for his/her trash and should contain it in a bag. Two-week-old onion rings in the ashtray are not a pretty sight.

When the **righteous** see God in action they'll **laugh**, they'll sing, they'll laugh and **sing for joy.**

PSALM 68:4 MSG

TOP **10** TIPS
for Cooking and Eating at Home

1. SET A REGULAR SHOPPING TIME TO KEEP YOUR KITCHEN WELL STOCKED.

2. MAKE YOUR SHOPPING LIST WITH SPECIFIC MEALS IN MIND.

3. BE REALISTIC: KEEP COOKING SIMPLE.

4. PULL THE CROCK POT OUT FROM THE BASEMENT SHELF AND USE IT.

5. REMEMBER, IT CAN BE JUST AS FAST TO COOK A SIMPLE DINNER AT HOME AS IT IS TO SIT IN A DRIVE-THRU LANE.

6. GET YOUR KIDS INVOLVED IN HELPING WITH THE DINNER ROUTINE.

7. IF YOU NEED MOTIVATION TO KEEP YOUR CAR FROM TURNING INTO THE DRIVE-THRU, JUST READ THE INGREDIENTS AND FAT/CALORIE STATS. NOT GOOD FOR ANYONE'S ARTERIES OR WEIGHT.

8. GIVE YOUR KIDS THE EXPERIENCE OF SITTING AROUND A DINNER TABLE WITH FAMILY.

9. REMEMBER THAT WHAT YOU SET AS THE STANDARD IS WHAT YOUR KIDS WILL FOLLOW—AND CARRY WITH THEM INTO ADULTHOOD.

10. THANK GOD FOR YOUR BLESSINGS IN PRAYER BEFORE MEALS.

CONSIDER
THIS!

As believers in Christ, we are compelled to show mercy to those we encounter—husbands, children, friends, strangers, and those who are unlovable. The Bible makes it clear that it isn't a Christian's place to judge, but to love selflessly and show mercy.

What's more, God's own gesture toward us provides a stirring example of how we should treat others. First Peter 1, verses 3-5 says, "Praise be to the God and Father of our Lord Jesus Christ! In his great mercy he has given us new birth into a living hope through the resurrection of Jesus Christ from the dead, and into an inheritance that can never perish, spoil or fade—kept in heaven for you, who through faith are shielded by God's power until the coming of the salvation that is ready to be revealed in the last time." Micah 6:8 asks, "What does the LORD require of you? To act justly and to love mercy and to walk humbly with your God."

BLESSED MERCY

According to a traditional Hebrew story, Abraham was sitting by his tent one evening when he saw an old man walking toward him. He could tell long before the man arrived that he was weary from age and his journey. Abraham rushed out to greet him, and then invited him into his tent. He washed the old man's feet and gave him something to drink and eat.

The old man immediately began eating without saying a prayer or invoking a blessing. Abraham asked him, "Don't you worship God?" The old traveler replied, "I worship fire only and reverence no other god." Upon hearing this, Abraham grabbed the old man by the shoulders and with indignation, threw him out of his tent into the cold night air.

The old man walked off into the night, and after he had gone, God called to His friend Abraham and asked where the stranger was. Abraham replied, "I forced him out of my tent because he did not worship You." The Lord responded, "I have suffered him these eighty years although he dishonors Me. Could you not endure him one night?"

Who today may need to experience your mercy as a tangible expression of the mercy God is extending to them?

> MERCY AMONG THE VIRTUES IS LIKE THE MOON AMONG THE STARS. . . . IT IS THE LIGHT THAT HOVERS ABOVE THE JUDGMENT SEAT.
>
> EDWIN HUBBEL CHAPIN

Mercy triumphs over judgment!

JAMES 2:13 NASB

THE POWER OF FORGIVENESS

Years after her experience in a Nazi Germany concentration camp, Corrie ten Boom found herself standing face-to-face with one of the most cruel and heartless German guards she had ever met in the camps. This man had humiliated and degraded both her and her sister, jeering at them and visually "raping" them as they stood in the delousing shower.

Now he stood before her with an outstretched hand, asking, "Will you forgive me?" Corrie said, "I stood there with coldness clutching at my heart, but I know that the will can function regardless of the temperature of the heart. I prayed, 'Jesus, help me!' Woodenly, mechanically, I thrust my hand into the one stretched out to me, and I experienced an incredible thing. The current started in my shoulder, raced down into my arm, and sprang into our clutched hands. Then this warm reconciliation seemed to flood my whole being, bringing tears to my eyes. 'I forgive you, brother,' I cried with my whole heart. For a long moment we grasped each other's hands, the former guard, the former prisoner. I have never known the love of God so intensely as I did in that moment!"

When we forgive we set a prisoner free—ourselves!

> "I CAN FORGIVE, BUT I CANNOT FORGET," IS ONLY ANOTHER WAY OF SAYING, "I WILL NOT FORGIVE." FORGIVENESS OUGHT TO BE LIKE A CANCELED NOTE—TORN IN TWO AND BURNED UP, SO THAT IT NEVER CAN BE SHOWN AGAINST ONE.
>
> HENRY WARD BEECHER

BE KIND ONE TO ANOTHER, TENDERHEARTED, FORGIVING ONE ANOTHER, AS GOD IN CHRIST HAS FORGIVEN YOU.

EPHESIANS 4:32 NRSV

WISE WORDS

[Jesus said,] "You have heard it was said, 'Love your neighbor and hate your enemy.' But I tell you: Love your enemies and pray for those who persecute you, that you may be sons of your Father in Heaven. He causes his sun to rise on the evil and the good, and sends rain on the righteous and the unrighteous. If you love those who love you, what reward will you get? Are not even the tax collectors doing that? And if you greet only your brothers, what are you doing more than others? Do not even pagans do that? Be perfect, therefore, as your heavenly Father is perfect."

MATTHEW 5:43-48

booklist

BRINGING UP BABY

MANY A WOMAN HAS felt "alone" during and after childbirth, but consider the true story of Martha Martin, wife of an Alaskan prospector in the 1920s.

While she was pregnant, her husband left her at their camp to run an errand to a neighboring island. A series of disasters struck almost immediately. First, an avalanche pinned her unconscious under a rock on the mountainside for several days. She managed to crawl back to their cabin and reset the broken bones she had suffered, making a splint for her leg and a cast for her arm. Then, a storm prevented her husband's return. Stranded, injured, alone, and with supplies almost gone, she quickly learned to be self-sufficient—killing animals for food

> I **remember** leaving the hospital ... thinking, "Wait, are they going to let me just walk off with him? I don't know beans about babies!"

and using their fur to make coverings for the coming baby. Bit by bit, she began burning portions of the cabin for heat.

Martha had never seen a child born before she went into two hard days of labor. But she kept her head and helped herself after her daughter finally arrived. She later baptized the infant Dannas. Several weeks later, some Indians appeared; and she finally had help until her husband, who had been caught on the other island, arrived. Her published diary was appropriately titled, *O Rugged Land of Gold.*

Babies aren't so hard to figure out. A little common sense and lots of love can cover just about everything.

If any of you is lacking in wisdom,
ask God, who gives to all generously and
ungrudgingly, and it will be given you.

JAMES 1:5 NRSV

"Think of the sacrifice your MOTHER had to make in order that you might live.

Think of the sacrifice GOD had to make that you and your mother might live."

DOING WHAT'S NECESSARY

In *My Mother Worked and I Turned Out Okay,* Katherine Wyse Goldman tells about Margaret, one of five children in a family during the 1930s and 1940s.

Margaret's mother left her alcoholic husband and took her children to live in a three-room apartment, which was all she could afford. Even at that, she had to work two jobs. Her night job was editing the company newspaper for the Pennsylvania Railroad from 10 p.m. to 7:30 a.m. The children would greet their mother by the curb when her trolley pulled up in the morning, and she'd get them ready for school. After only a couple of hours of sleep, she'd go to her day job from 10 a.m. to 4 p.m., at which time her children would greet her at the same curb.

After a light supper, the children did their homework as quietly as possible so their mother could get a few more hours of sleep. Margaret said of her mother: "Mother never had a day off both jobs at the same time. My grandmother wanted to put us in foster homes, but my mother said no, that she could do it. She'd tell us the way we lived was temporary."

What wonderful wisdom to remember about any of the hardships we experience as mothers—this, too, is only temporary!

Who's Who: *Esther*

Esther was a beautiful Jewish woman who married the powerful King Xerxes. Esther's parents had been killed when she was a young girl, and she was adopted by her father's cousin, Mordecai. When Esther was in the running to become queen, Mordecai forbade her to reveal her nationality and family background, so Xerxes had no idea she was Jewish.

King Xerxes appointed a less-than-scrupulous man, Haman, to the highest position in his court. Haman had a grudge against Mordecai and a great chip on his shoulder regarding the Jewish people. Haman convinced the king that the Jewish people were not obeying his laws and to decree that all the Jews should be killed.

Mordecai sent word to Esther and asked her to help. Esther didn't ignore him. She didn't dissolve into tears. Instead, she immediately began to analyze the situation. After corresponding with her uncle, she gave this direction to him, "Go, gather together all the Jews who are in Susa, and fast for me. Do not eat or drink for three days, night or day. I and my maids will fast as you do. When this is done, I will go to the king, even though it is against the law. And if I perish, I perish."

God honored the fast and prayer, and Esther was able to approach the king. Still, Esther used wisdom and tact in achieving her ends. The book of Esther recounts the remarkable story of this brave woman who saved her people by prayer, ingenuity, and action.

A CHILD'S TAKE

A salesman telephoned a household, and a four-year-old boy answered. He said, "May I speak to your mother, please?"

The little boy replied, "She's in the shower right now and can't come to the phone."

The salesman asked, "Well, is anyone else at home?"

"Yes," the boy said, "my sister is here."

"Well, OK," the salesman continued. "May I speak to her, please?"

"I guess so," the boy said. "I'll go get her."

At this point the salesman heard a clunk as the boy laid down the receiver. This was followed by a very long silence on the phone.

Finally the little boy came back on the line and said, "Are you still there?"

"Yes," the salesman said, trying hard to sound patient, "I thought you were going to put your sister on the phone."

The boy replied, "I tried, mister. But she's sound asleep, and I couldn't lift her out of her crib."

> **Any time**
> a child can
> be seen but
> not heard,
> it's a shame
> to wake him.

If they obey and serve Him, they shall spend

lighten up

One broadcast of the radio show "This American Life" featured the following story:

Two boys were talking at school about the Tooth Fairy. Each was at the tender age when smiles become marked with the gaping holes left by the absence of baby teeth. The first boy, Joey Emerson, said to the other, "Guess what! Last night, I saw my father come into my room, take my tooth, and put the money under my pillow."

The other boy went home from school that day, stormed into the house and announced to his mom, "Well . . . I know who the Tooth Fairy is."

"Oh, you do?" answered his mom, who was certain this would mark the end of the era of belief for her child. "Who is it?"

"It's Mr. Emerson," the boy replied earnestly.

A mother was telling her little girl what her own childhood was like: "We used to skate outside on a pond. I had a swing made from a tire; it hung from a tree in our front yard. We rode our pony. We picked wild raspberries in the woods."

The little girl was wide-eyed, taking this in. At last she said, "I sure wish I'd gotten to know you sooner!"

their days in prosperity . . . and joy. JOB 36:11 AMP

Trivia

Fun

Did you know that the word smile is used only three times in the Bible, all in the same book of the Old Testament? In which OT book do you think it's used? Is it:

A. Song of Songs
B. Job
C. Ruth?

Think about the most unlikely place for the word "smile" to be used, and you've guessed it right. "Smile" or "smiled" is used in Job 9:27; 10:3, and 29:24. Now there's a little bit of biblical irony for you.

LIGHT IN A SMILE

Beautiful as seemed **mama's face,**
it became incomparably more
lovely when she **smiled,** and seemed
to **enliven** everything about her.

LEO TOLSTOY

For more than a century, the majestic statue titled *Liberty Enlightening the World* has towered near the entrance to New York Harbor as a symbol of America's freedom.

The famous sculptor of the statue, Bartholdi, spent twenty years supervising the construction of his masterpiece. He personally helped raise the four million dollars needed to pay for the statue, which was presented by France as a gift to the United States. When the fund-raising program for the statue lagged, Bartholdi pledged his own private fortune to keep the project funded and practically impoverished himself in the process.

At the start, when Bartholdi was seeking a model on whom to pattern "Liberty," he received a great deal of advice from art experts. Most of the leading authorities advised him to find a grand heroic figure as his pattern. After examining countless heroes, however, Bartholdi chose as his model his own mother. Just as no other statue in the world so eloquently lights the way to freedom, so no other woman so beautifully lighted Bartholdi's own world.

Remember, your children are watching even the very expressions of your face—be sure a fair amount of the time it wears a smile.

The joy of the LORD
is your strength.

NEHEMIAH 8:10 KJV

POWER IN PATIENCE

> WE NEED TO BE **PATIENT** WITH OUR **CHILDREN** IN THE **SAME** WAY **GOD** IS **PATIENT** WITH **US.**
>
> RENEE JORDAN

ONE OF THE most beautiful descriptions of patience in all of classic literature is this from Bishop Horne:

"Patience is the guardian of faith, the preserver of peace, the cherisher of love, the teacher of humility. Patience governs the flesh, strengthens the spirit, sweetens the temper, stifles anger, extinguishes envy, subdues pride: she bridles the tongue, restrains the hand, tramples upon temptations, endures persecutions, consummates martyrdom.

"Patience produces unity in the church, loyalty in the state, harmony in families and societies: she comforts the poor, and moderates the rich; she makes us humble in prosperity, cheerful in adversity, unmoved by calumny [slander] and reproach; she teaches us to forgive those who have injured us, and to be the first in asking forgiveness of those whom we have injured; she delights the faithful, and invites the unbelieving; she adorns the woman, and approves the man; she is beautiful in either sex and every age. . . .

"She rides not in the whirlwind and stormy tempest of passion, but her throne is the humble and contrite heart, and her kingdom is the kingdom of peace."

Remember, when the opportunity arises to be patient with your child, consider how you would want God to respond to you in a similar circumstance.

Those with good sense are slow to anger, and it is their glory to overlook an offense.

PROVERBS 19:11 NRSV

TOP 10 TIPS for Keeping Your Cool with Your Kids

1. HAVE A CATCH PHRASE THAT YOU REPEAT TO YOURSELF WHEN YOU'RE FEELING PUSHED BY YOUR KIDS, LIKE, "I'M THE ADULT."

2. SEPARATE YOURSELF FROM YOUR CHILDREN FOR A FEW MINUTES TO REGAIN YOUR COMPOSURE.

3. PRACTICE KEEPING AN EVEN TONE WHEN YOU DISCIPLINE YOUR KIDS. YELLING CAN ESCALATE THE SITUATION EVEN FURTHER.

4. REALIZE IF YOU'RE FEELING ESPECIALLY TIRED OR STRESSED, AND ADJUST YOUR EXPECTATIONS AND RESPONSES ACCORDINGLY.

5. THINK THROUGH THE COMMON "HOT BUTTONS" AND HOW YOU WILL RESPOND.

6. DON'T BE AFRAID TO TELL YOUR KIDS THAT YOU NEED A LITTLE TIME TO THINK ABOUT A SITUATION BEFORE YOU DEAL WITH IT.

7. DECIDE WHICH THINGS YOU WILL NOT BEND ON, AND STAY CONSISTENT.

8. TAKE TIME AWAY FROM THE KIDS AND DO SOMETHING ENJOYABLE.

9. POST BIBLE VERSES OR QUOTES THAT CAN HELP YOU KEEP PERSPECTIVE AS YOU'RE INTERACTING WITH YOUR KIDS.

10. ASK GOD FOR HELP—ALL DAY LONG.

CONSIDER
THIS!

Have you introduced the Word of God to your children? It's never too early. They may not have the reasoning ability to grasp greater truths or complex mysteries, but they can begin to derive the security and hope that comes with biblical truths.

The idea that "God made me and the world around me" can provide a child with the beginnings of sense of purpose. Truths like, "God is greater than anyone or anything on earth, and He is always near," can give a sense of comfort and help children deal with fear. "Jesus loves me" is just the beginning sentence for the greatest story ever told and the single most important factor in the life of your child—salvation, by the grace of God through Jesus Christ.

Don't wait. Make the Bible the most important and well-read book in your home.

MIX-INFORMATION

A group of four-year-olds were gathered in a Sunday school class one spring. Their teacher asked them, "Does anyone know what today is?"

A little girl held up her hand and said, "It's Palm Sunday." "Wonderful!" exclaimed the teacher. "Now does anyone know what next Sunday is?" No answer. Finally, as if a light had just come on, the same little girl shouted, "I do! Next Sunday is Easter."

The teacher responded, "That's fantastic!" Ready to drive her point home, she asked, "Now, does anyone know what makes next Sunday Easter?"

FINGERPRINTING CHILDREN IS A GOOD IDEA. IT WILL SETTLE THE QUESTION AS TO WHO USED THE GUEST TOWEL IN THE BATHROOM.

At this the little girl jumped up and said, "Yes! Next Sunday is Easter because Jesus rose from the grave." Before the teacher could congratulate her on yet another correct answer, the little girl continued, "But if He sees His shadow, He has to go back in for seven weeks."

Listen closely to what others tell you. Weigh it against what you know to be God's truth. Information is different from truth. It comes in varying degrees of accuracy, whereas truth comes in only one package, labeled: the whole truth and nothing but the truth.

Test everything that is said
to be sure it is true,
and if it is, then accept it.

1 THESSALONIANS 5:21 TLB

SEEING IS BECOMING

Behavioral pediatrician John Obedzinski saw two types of families in his practice. On one hand were well-educated parents who raised their children "progressively," allowing their children total freedom of choice and expression. Their children were often sullen, arrogant, and totally self-absorbed. On the other hand were parents who were harsh disciplinarians and who made all their children's decisions. These children were often rebellious.

WHEN WE SET AN EXAMPLE OF HONESTY OUR CHILDREN WILL BE HONEST. WHEN WE ENCIRCLE THEM WITH LOVE THEY WILL BE LOVING. WHEN WE PRACTICE TOLERANCE THEY WILL BE TOLERANT. WHEN WE MEET LIFE WITH LAUGHTER AND A TWINKLE IN OUR EYE THEY WILL DEVELOP A SENSE OF HUMOR.

Obedzinski set out to study resilient, happy families that seemed to weather life's ups and downs with loyalty and love. In doing so, he found these seven traits to be common:

• the children know their place—a family is not a democracy, and children do not have total freedom,

• the family values tradition and keeps treasured rituals, especially at holiday time,

• family members admit their mistakes openly,

• family members acknowledge their differences and try to accommodate them,

• children are taught to compete against each other in ways that are fair and friendly,

• children have chores and responsibilities, and

• family members tease one another and laugh at their own foibles, but the humor is never malicious.

TEACH BELIEVERS WITH YOUR LIFE: BY WORD, BY DEMEANOR, BY LOVE, BY FAITH, BY INTEGRITY.

1 TIMOTHY 4:12 MSG

WISE WORDS

The childhood shows the man,
As morning shows the day. Be famous then
By wisdom; as thy empire must extend,
So let extend thy mind o'er all the world.

JOHN MILTON

Listen, my son, accept what I say, and the years of your life
will be many. I guide you in the way of wisdom and lead you
along straight paths. When you walk, your steps will not be
hampered; when you run, you will not stumble. Hold on to
instruction, do not let it go; guard it well, for it is your life.
PROVERBS 4:10-13

HOW Do YOU MEASURE Up?

Five Ways to Know If You're Putting a Shine on Your Child

1. In an argument with other kids, you always assume your child is right.
2. If your child expresses displeasure, you seek to change circumstances immediately.
3. You allow your child to express himself at any time, even if you're having a conversation with another adult.
4. You believe yours is the cutest, brightest, most charming child ever begotten who could at any moment sing and dance their way directly to Broadway.
5. You are certain America would love to watch a reality TV show based solely on the antics of your little darling.

Five Reality Checks for All Parents

1. Always taking your child's side sends a message that they're never wrong, or shouldn't admit wrongdoing. It also makes them weak in future conflict-resolution when you're not there to take their side.
2. It's okay for your child to struggle a bit to adjust to a new situation or to face discomfort. It's not cruel—this is preparing them to be more tolerant and flexible when it comes to the not-so-fun stuff of life.
3. When you let your child interrupt whenever, wherever, it gives them a false sense of importance. Plus, it's a bit rude.
4. Your baby is the apple of your eye with their own wonderful strengths and talents that should be noticed and cultivated, but they're not perfect. Make sure you're not putting undue pressure on your child. Let them develop the natural talents God has given to them—not the ones you'd like them to have.
5. You could watch your home videos, laugh, cry, and see them again and again. The rest of the world, with the exception of grandparents or other people whose children are in your videos, doesn't share your enthusiasm. It's nothing personal.

EYE OF THE BEHOLDER

THERE IS ONLY ONE PRETTY CHILD IN THE WORLD, AND EVERY MOTHER HAS IT.

During World War I, one of the most popular songs was that about a rookie named Jim. The song recounts a mother telling a friend how she stood on the sidewalk and watched her son's regiment march by. Oh, how proud she was of him! But, as Jim came marching by, she noticed something amiss. All the other young men were putting down their right foot when Jim was putting down his left. When all the others were going right-left, Jim was marching left-right.

She concludes, as many a proud mother might:

"Were you there?

And tell me did you notice?

They were all out of step but Jim!"

Mothers should never live in denial about their children's mistakes or faults. Facing weaknesses, and helping a child to face them, is one of the best ways to help a child grow strong. At the same time, the Scriptures tell us that "love covers a multitude of sins" (1 Peter 4:8). In truly loving a person, we are not to deny their flaws, but to say instead, "I choose to love this person in spite of their mistakes and flaws and to focus instead on all the things that make this person beautiful, wonderful, and lovable!"

[God] hath made every thing beautiful in his time.

ECCLESIASTES 3:11 KJV

MONUMENTAL TASK

Columnist Abigail Van Buren published a Parent's Prayer in her "Dear Abby" column. It read, in part:

"O, heavenly Father, make me a better parent. Teach me to understand my children, to listen patiently to what they have to say, and to answer all their questions kindly. Keep me from interrupting them or contradicting them. Make me as courteous to them as I would have them be to me. Forbid that I should ever laugh at their mistakes, or resort to shame or ridicule when they displease me. May I never punish them for my own selfish satisfaction or to show my power.

> **Parenthood** is a partnership with God . . . you are working with the Creator of the universe in shaping human character and determining destiny. RUTH VAUGHN

"Let me not tempt my child to lie or steal. And guide me hour by hour that I may demonstrate by all I say and do that honesty produces happiness. Reduce, I pray, the meanness in me. And when I am out of sorts, help me, O Lord, to hold my tongue. May I ever be mindful that my children are children and I should not expect of them the judgment of adults.

"Let me not rob them of the opportunity to wait on themselves and to make decisions. Bless me with the bigness to give them all their reasonable requests, and the courage to deny them privileges I know will do them harm. . . . And fit me, O Lord, to be loved and respected and imitated by my children. Amen."

We are labourers **together** with God.

1 CORINTHIANS 3:9 KJV

No mother is perfect—and if she believes she is, that's her primary flaw! Think honestly about some things you'd like to change about yourself, things that you believe would make you a better parent—inward characteristics or responses such as:

- Quick temper
- Impatience
- Perfectionist tendencies or lack of motivation

Pray specifically about the characteristics you've identified, saying: "Father, I know You want me to be the best person and mom I possibly can. Thank You for working in my heart and in my life to bring about the changes that You desire. I pray that You will help me become a better parent. With Your help, I will endeavor to live above my tendency to _____." Amen.

DIAMONDS IN THE ROUGH

A NUMBER OF YEARS AGO, a magnificent diamond was found in an African mine. It was presented to the king of England to be part of his crown. The king, in turn, sent it to Amsterdam to be cut. The stone was put into the hands of an expert lapidary. For weeks, he studied its quality, its defects, its cleavage lines, its most minute details. Drawings and models were made of the stone. Then the day came when he cut a notch in this rock of priceless value, and struck a hard blow with one of his instruments. In less than a second, the superb jewel lay on his table in two pieces.

> **Many parents** are finding out that a pat on the back helps develop character—if given often enough, early enough, and low enough.

Was his blow a mistake? Far from it. In striking the rough, uncut stone with such precision, he brought forth from it two magnificent gems with perfect shape, radiance, and splendor. From a raw stone, he had created two priceless jewels. Rather than destroying the diamond, he had redeemed it to its full value.

The discipline we give our children must be done with like precision, thoughtfulness, and toward the same end—the bringing out of our child's best qualities so he or she might become a radiant "living stone" in God's eternal crown.

A refusal to correct is a refusal to love; love your children by disciplining them.

PROVERBS 13:24 MSG

| new insights into ageless questions

There are so many theories out there on the right way
to discipline children. As a Christian mom, I find this quite
confusing. What does the Bible have to say?

You're right—there are more methods than a mother can weed through.
What seems to be important is to settle on a framework for discipline,
certain specific principles from which you can shape your actions when
you're faced with a disciplining challenge. Scripture points parents to
several of these guiding principles:

1. Provide consistent discipline and instruction (Proverbs 19:18).

2. Teach your children about God, through His Word
   (Deuteronomy 31:13).

3. Be a Godly example to your children (2 Chronicles 17:3).

4. Act in love, not anger (Colossians 3:21).

5. Discipline and then move on—forgive and don't hold grievances
   over your child's head (Colossians 3:13).

A MOTHER'S REACH

DURING A SPECIAL PROGRAM at church, a little girl was to recite the Scripture she had been assigned for the occasion. When she got in front of the crowd, however, the sight of hundreds of eyes peering at her caused her to have a bout of stage fright. She completely forgot her verse and was unable to utter a single word.

Her mother, sitting in the front row, leaned forward, and after several attempts, finally got her daughter's attention. She moved her lips and gestured, but her daughter didn't seem to comprehend what she was doing. Finally, the mother whispered the opening phrase of the verse she was to recite, "I am the light of the world."

The little girl's face lit up, and she smiled with confidence. "My mother is the light of the world!" she announced boldly.

Her words brought a smile to the face of each audience member, of course, and yet upon reflection, most had to admit that she had declared an eloquent truth. A mother is the light of her child's world.

Let your light shine brightly today on your child's behalf!

lighten up

With all of the technical and mechanical advances we enjoy, one would think that the work of motherhood would be a snap—like Judy Jetson, of the cartoon series *The Jetsons,* with her helpful robot housekeepers. Any mother knows that this is not the case. Here's what one mother, Ruth Schwarz Cowan, had to say about modern "advances":

Modern labor-saving devices eliminated drudgery, not labor. Before industrialization, women fed, clothed, and nursed their families by preparing (with the help of their husbands and children) food, clothing, and medication. In the post-industrial age, women feed, clothe, and nurse their families (without much direct assistance from anyone else) by cooking, cleaning, driving, shopping, and waiting.

"My mother was the source from which I derived the guiding principles of my life."

JOHN WESLEY

I also am of Christ. 1 CORINTHIANS 11:1

DISASTER AREA

CLEANING YOUR HOUSE WHILE YOUR KIDS ARE STILL GROWING IS LIKE SHOVELING THE WALK BEFORE IT STOPS SNOWING.

PHILLIS DILLER

ELINOR Goulding Smith offers this analysis of a child's room: "The child's room is a sight to make strong men faint, and induces in mothers a condition characterized by trembling, pallor, dysphasia, weakness. . . . The room is characterized by litter to a depth of two to three feet, except under the bed where it is perhaps only six inches deep. You can see no article of furniture, each being buried completely, and emerging as simply a higher mound of rubbish. You once, many years before, saw an occasional bureau top (let me see, was it maple?) or a desk top (birch—I think) but alas, they are only a memory now.

"A few bits of furniture stick up above the level of the rubbish—the very top of a desk lamp protrudes above a mountain of papers, books, crayons, hedge shears, gym sneakers, the remains of a tongue sandwich, two peach pits, a camera, a microscope, some jars of extremely aromatic pond water, a deck of marked cards, coping saw, overdue library books, bicycle tire pumps, a Siamese fighting fish no longer in the prime of life who lives in the bottom half of a cider jug, and so on . . . right up to the top of the desk lamp. You look at the top of the lamp happily. 'At last,' you say, as you totter across the room, 'a landmark!'"

A cheerful heart
is a good medicine.

PROVERBS 17:22 NRSV

TOP 10 TIPS for Getting a Kid to Keep a Clean Room

1. START MINIMIZING CLUTTER IN YOUR CHILD'S ROOM EARLY.

2. FOR YOUNGER KIDS, SWITCH OUT THEIR TOYS AND BOOKS EVERY FEW WEEKS TO LIMIT CLUTTER.

3. HAVE YOUR KIDS HELP YOU CLEAN UP TOYS WHEN THEY'RE VERY YOUNG, AND BE CONSISTENT IN GETTING THEM TO HELP.

4. WITH OLDER KIDS, DECIDE BETWEEN YOU WHAT'S ACCEPTABLE, AND THEN ENFORCE IT.

5. GIVE KIDS WHO HAVE TROUBLE STAYING ORGANIZED THE MEANS TO DO SO WITH FUN STORAGE OR FILING OPTIONS.

6. LET KIDS CHOOSE THE DÉCOR FOR THEIR ROOMS SO THEY HAVE A SENSE OF PRIDE AND OWNERSHIP.

7. ATTACH CONDITIONS, LIKE "NO CLEAN ROOM, NO COMPUTER GAMES."

8. IF A CHILD HAS A PROBLEM OR JUST DOESN'T CARE ABOUT THE MESS, CHECK IN MORE OFTEN, BEFORE THE ROOM CAN BE DECLARED A DISASTER AREA.

9. TIE A CLEAN ROOM IN WITH A CHILD'S WEEKLY ALLOWANCE, IF AN ALLOWANCE IS PART OF YOUR ROUTINE.

10. REMIND YOUR KIDS THAT GOD HAS BLESSED THEM WITH THE MEANS FOR HAVING ALL THIS WONDERFUL STUFF—AND IT COULD EASILY DISAPPEAR IF IT'S NOT TREATED RESPECTFULLY.

CONSIDER
THIS!

What Is Prayer?
Prayer is the soul's sincere desire,
Uttered or unexpressed;
The motion of a hidden fire
That trembles in the breast.

JAMES MONTGOMERY

Likewise the Spirit helps us in our weakness; for we do not know how to pray as we ought, but that very Spirit intercedes with sighs too deep for words. And God, who searches the heart, knows what is the mind of the Spirit, because the Spirit intercedes for the saints according to the will of God.

ROMANS 8:26-27 NRSV

NOT IN VAIN

When W. P. L. Mackay was seventeen, he left his humble Scottish home to attend college. His mother gave him a Bible in which she wrote his name and a verse of Scripture. Unfortunately, college was only the beginning of a downhill lifestyle for him. At one point he pawned the Bible to get money for whiskey. His mother, however, prayed for him until she died.

> EVERY MOTHER IS LIKE MOSES. SHE DOES NOT ENTER THE PROMISED LAND. SHE PREPARES A WORLD SHE WILL NOT SEE.
>
> POPE PAUL VI

Eventually, Mackay became a doctor. While working in a hospital, he encountered a dying patient who asked repeatedly for his "book." After the man died, Mackay searched the hospital room to find what book it was that had been so important to him. He was surprised to find the very Bible he had once pawned!

Mackay went to his office and stared again at the familiar writing of his mother. He thumbed through the pages, reading the many verses his mother had underscored in hopes her son might heed them in his life. After many hours of reading and reflection, Mackay prayed to God for mercy. The physician later became a minister. And the Book he once had treated so lightly became his most precious possession.

You may not live to see how your children will turn out. But you can trust that nothing you do for their spiritual wholeness will have been in vain!

The LORD said to him, "This is the land I promised on oath to Abraham, Isaac and Jacob. . . . I have let you see it with your eyes, but you will not cross over into it."

DEUTERONOMY 34:4

GODLY HERITAGE

His mother, Eliza, was an intelligent woman with strong common sense and straitlaced conduct. A disciplinarian, she was devoutly religious and a believer in hard work and thrift. Her strong will and deep piety gave her a remarkable serenity, which she transmitted to her son, John. A diligent and serious student, John was trained by his mother in matters of piety, neatness, and industry. Attendance at church and Sunday school was weekly.

His father was full of the joy of life and loved song, talk, and sociability. He taught John to develop his innate gift for business. William was as anxious as Eliza that all their children grow up self-reliant, honest, keen-witted, and dependable. John recalled later that both of his parents were examples of courtesy and patience. He said, "I cannot remember to have heard the voices of either Father or Mother raised in anger or complaint in speaking to any of us."

William and Eliza also instilled in their son a rich heritage of giving to church and charities, the gifts being made from their childhood earnings. In all, William and Eliza gave their son, John D. Rockefeller, a happy childhood— a gift he valued throughout his life far more than the millions of dollars he made.

> A HAPPY CHILDHOOD IS ONE OF THE BEST GIFTS THAT PARENTS HAVE IT IN THEIR POWER TO BESTOW.
>
> MARY CHOLMONDELEY

DO NOT WITHHOLD GOOD FROM THOSE TO WHOM IT IS DUE, WHEN IT IS IN THE POWER OF YOUR HAND TO DO SO.

PROVERBS 3:27 NKJV

WISE WORDS

Rejoice in the Lord always. I will say it again:
Rejoice! Let your gentleness be evident to all.
The Lord is near. Do not be anxious about anything, but in everything, by prayer and petition,
with thanksgiving, present your requests to
God. And the peace of God, which transcends
all understanding, will guard your hearts and
your minds in Christ Jesus. Finally, brothers,
whatever is true, whatever is noble, whatever is
right, whatever is pure, whatever is lovely, whatever is admirable—if anything is excellent or
praiseworthy—think about such things.
Whatever you have learned or received or heard
from me, or seen in me—put it into practice.
And the God of peace will be with you.

PHILIPPIANS 4:4-9

booklist

read more about it... to your children

- *Jesus Loves the Little Children & Jesus Loves Me*
  by Debby Anderson

- *I'll Love You Forever*
  by Robert Munsch

- *Guess How Much I Love You*
  by Sam McBratney

- *You Are Special*
  by Max Lucado

- *The Beginner's Bible*
  by Karyn Henley

BY INVITATION

MARGARET BOURKE-White, one of the innovators of the photo essay in the field of photojournalism, was one of the first four staff photographers of *Life* magazine when it began in 1936. She was also the first woman photographer ever attached to U. S. armed forces in World War II. From early years, Margaret knew that she was counted as a "gift" to her parents. She recalls her mother telling her, "Margaret, you can always be proud that you were invited into the world."

In her autobiography, aptly titled *Portrait of Myself,* she writes: "I don't know where she got this fine philosophy that children should come because they were wanted and should not be the result of accidents. . . . When each of her own three children was on the way, Mother would say to those closest to her, 'I don't know whether this will be a boy or girl, and I don't care. But this child was invited into the world and it will be a wonderful child.' She was explicit about the invitation and believed the child should be the welcomed result of a known and definite act of love between man and woman."

Have you told your child today that they are a gift—a child you wanted and "invited" into the world?

What good news that is to a child's ears!

> **A child is** a gift whose worth cannot be measured except by the heart.
>
> THERESA ANN HUNT

Behold, children are a gift of the Lord; the fruit of the womb is a reward.

PSALM 127:3 NASB

"Each loving act says loud and CLEAR, 'I love you. God loves you. I care. God cares.'"

JOYCE HEINRICH AND ANNETTE LaPLACA

ACTS OF LOVE

When Rose Kennedy died at age 104, the world lost one of the most dedicated and famous mothers of this century. She was mother to nine children, among them a former United States President and Attorney General, and a current United States Senator.

In spite of her own marital challenges, the birth of a mentally challenged child, and the early deaths of four of her children, Rose Kennedy lived a life of faith and strength before her children and grandchildren. At her funeral, her son Ted put into perspective the considerable impact that she had on the lives of her family members—with actions both great and small—conveying to her children her love and care and God's love and care:

"She sustained us in the saddest times.

"Her faith in God was the greatest gift she gave us.

"She was ambitious not only for our success but for our souls. From our youth we remember how, with effortless ease, she could bandage a cut, dry a tear, recite from memory 'The Midnight Ride of Paul Revere,' and spot a hole in a sock from a hundred yards away."

Great mothers don't always bear children who achieve greatness in the eyes of the world, but great mothers always do convey great love.

Who's Who:

Deaconess Phoebe

When it comes to notable women of the Bible, the name "Phoebe" probably wouldn't come to mind. She is mentioned only once—in the book of Romans. Paul writes in his closing comments to the Roman church, "I commend to you our sister Phoebe, a servant (or deaconess) of the church in Cenchrea. I ask you to receive her in the Lord in a way worthy of the saints and to give her any help she may need from you, for she has been a great help to many people, including me."

Phoebe is first in a list of many people to whom Paul sends greetings and, to some, commendations. This would indicate that he wanted the people of that church to know he held Phoebe in high esteem. His direction to give Phoebe anything she needed shows trust in her judgment and character. One can only assume that she was a strong woman who could hold her own, moving from city to city, helping those in a church that was struggling to find its way. Some biblical scholars believe that Phoebe may have traveled to Rome and delivered Paul's letter to the church there.

Little is known about Phoebe's life, but what is known about her character makes her an example for all believers as a person of notable kindness and strength.

UNFLAGGING PATIENCE

ACCORDING TO A FABLE, a woman showed up one snowy morning at 5 a.m. at the home of an "examiner" of "suitable mother" candidates. Ushered in, she was asked to sit for three hours past her appointment time before she was interviewed. The first question given to her in the interview was, "Can you spell?" Yes, she said. "Then spell 'cook.'" The woman responded, "C-O-O-K."

The examiner then asked, "Do you know anything about numbers?" The woman replied, "Yes, sir, some things." The examiner said, "Please add two plus two." The candidate replied, "Four."

"Fine," announced the examiner. "We'll be in touch." At the board meeting of examiners held the next day, the examiner reported that the woman had all the qualifications to be a fine mother. He said, "First I tested her on self-denial, making her arrive at five in the morning on a snowy day. Then I tested her on patience. She waited three hours without complaint. Third, I tested her on temper, asking her questions a child could answer. She never showed indignation or anger. She'll make a fine mother." And all on the board agreed.

> ## lighten up
>
> Motherhood is the second oldest profession in the world. It never questions age, height, religious preference, health, political affiliation, citizenship, morality, ethnic background, marital status, economic level, convenience, or previous experience.
>
> ERMA BOMBECK

Being strengthened with all power according to his glorious
COLOSSIANS 1:11 NIV

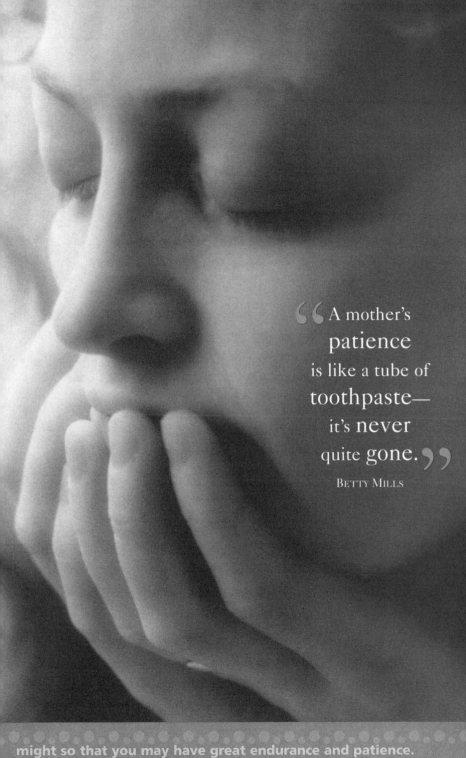

A mother's patience is like a tube of **toothpaste**— it's **never** quite **gone.**

BETTY MILLS

might so that you may have great endurance and patience.

Trivia

Fun

The Bible clearly teaches people of God to pray—often (in fact, constantly), humbly, hopefully, and with unwavering faith. Ephesians 6:18 says, "Pray in the Spirit on all occasions with all kinds of prayers and requests. With this in mind, be alert and always keep on praying for all the saints."

When does the Bible say man began to pray to God?

A. When Adam was in the Garden of Eden.
B. After Cain killed Abel and Seth was born to Eve.
C. The time of Noah, prior to the construction of the Ark.

The Bible says in Genesis 4:25-26: "Adam lay with his wife again, and she gave birth to a son and named him Seth, saying, 'God has granted me another child in place of Abel, since Cain killed him.' Seth also had a son, and he named him Enosh. At that time men began to call on the name of the LORD."

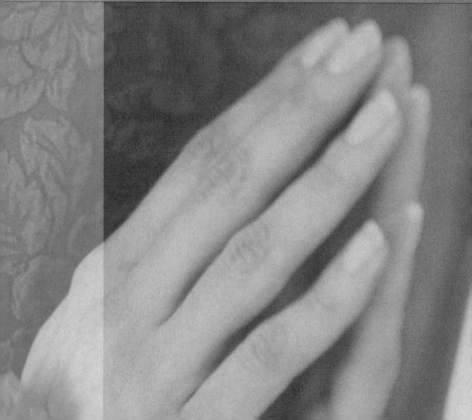

THE REACH OF PRAYER

Many a **man** has kept
straight because his
mother bent her **knees.**

A woman with hot tears flowing down her face, praying for him—that was what John remembered, even after he went off to sea and later became a very wicked man who traded in slaves. But John's mother believed in two things, the power of prayer and the power of God to reform her son and give him a heart for the ministry. God answered the prayer by working a miracle in the heart of John Newton.

John Newton, the drunken sailor became John Newton, the sailor-preacher [who wrote the words to "Amazing Grace."] Among the thousands of men and women he brought to Christ was Thomas Scott . . . [who] used both his pen and voice to lead thousands of unbelieving hearts to Christ, among them William Cowper . . . [who] in a moment of inspiration wrote "There Is a Fountain Filled with Blood." And this song has brought countless thousands to the Man who died on Calvary. All this resulted because a mother took God at His word and prayed that her son's heart might become as white as the soapsuds in the washtub.—adapted from *Springs in the Valley* by Mrs. Charles E. Cowman.

The earnest prayer
of a righteous man
has great power and
wonderful results.

JAMES 5:16 TLB

MISBEHAVIN'

> PARENTS MUST GET ACROSS THE **IDEA** THAT, "I **LOVE** YOU **ALWAYS,** BUT SOMETIMES I **DO NOT LOVE** YOUR **BEHAVIOR."**
>
> AMY VANDERBILT

LITTLE EDWARD misbehaved during dinner one evening. His father, a strict but fair disciplinarian, reprimanded him. Still, Eddy didn't change his ways. The father finally said, "Eddy, if you do not behave, you will be sent to your room and there will be no more food for you tonight."

Eddy didn't listen, but continued to misbehave. At that, he was ordered to march to his bedroom, change into his nightclothes, and climb into bed.

As he lay in bed, Eddy's every thought turned to food. He couldn't remember ever having felt more hungry, or more alone or alienated from the family. He began to cry. Then he heard a noise on the stairs and footsteps walking closer and closer to his room. The door opened and in came his father.

Closing the door behind him, he came over to Eddy's bed and said, "I love you, Eddy, and I've come to spend the night with you."

Not all behavior is worthy of applause. But every moment of a child's life and every ounce of a child's being is worthy of love.

Those whom I love,
I reprove and discipline; be zealous
therefore, and repent.

REVELATION 3:19 NASB

TOP **10** TIPS for Disciplining Kids

1. DON'T GIVE AN ULTIMATUM THAT WILL BE HARD TO FOLLOW THROUGH WITH.

2. REFRAIN FROM NEGOTIATING WITH YOUR CHILDREN. IT'S THEIR WAY OF TRYING TO GAIN CONTROL.

3. AS THE BIBLE SAYS IN MATTHEW 5:27, "LET YOUR 'YES' BE 'YES,' AND YOUR 'NO' BE 'NO.'"

4. EVALUATE WHAT MEANS OF CORRECTION WORKS FOR EACH OF YOUR CHILDREN.

5. TRY TO SET YOUR KIDS UP FOR SUCCESS, EVEN IN THE MIDST OF DISCIPLINING THEM. DON'T PLACE A DIRECTIVE ON THEM THAT YOU KNOW THEY CAN'T ACCOMPLISH.

6. STAY CALM, IF AT ALL POSSIBLE.

7. TALK TO YOUR KIDS ABOUT WHAT'S "GONE DOWN" AND WHY YOU SCOLDED OR PUNISHED THEM.

8. IF THE CIRCUMSTANCES ALLOW, INSTEAD OF TELLING YOUR CHILD, "NO," POINT HIM TO AN ALTERNATIVE ACTION OR ACTIVITY.

9. BE PATIENT, AND KEEP IN MIND THAT CERTAIN BEHAVIORS ARE PART OF DIFFERENT STAGES IN YOUR CHILD'S DEVELOPMENT.

10. PRAY THAT GOD WILL GIVE YOU EVERY BIT OF WISDOM AND PERSEVERANCE POSSIBLE AS YOU WORK TO INSTRUCT YOUR CHILDREN TO DO AND BE AND LIVE RIGHTLY AND JUSTLY.

CONSIDER THIS!

Christ's parable in Matthew 18:10-14 illustrates the value God places on the individual soul. Jesus says, "See that you do not look down on one of these little ones. For I tell you that their angels in heaven always see the face of my Father in heaven. What do you think? If a man owns a hundred sheep, and one of them wanders away, will he not leave the ninety-nine on the hills and go to look for the one that wandered off? And if he finds it, I tell you the truth, he is happier about that one sheep than about the ninety-nine that did not wander off. In the same way your Father in heaven is not willing that any of these little ones should be lost."

Teach your children to value themselves and others not only for who God made them to be, but because God values them beyond measure.

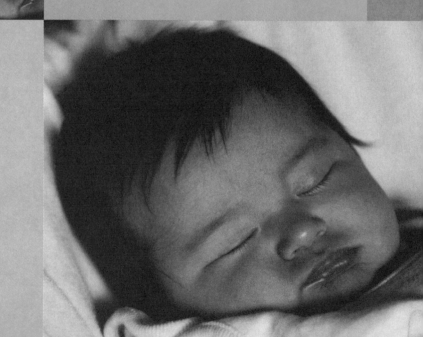

A CASE FOR LIFE

A professor in a world-acclaimed medical school once posed this medical situation—and ethical problem—to his students: "Here's the family history: The father has syphilis. The mother has TB. They already have had four children. The first is blind. The second had died. The third is deaf. The fourth has TB. Now the mother is pregnant again. The parents come to you for advice. They are willing to have an abortion, if you decide they should. What do you say?"

The students gave various individual opinions, and then the professor asked them to break into small groups for "consultation." All of the groups came back to report that they would recommend abortion.

"Congratulations," the professor said. "You just took the life of Beethoven!"

A woman helps create the body of her child, and as her child grows, she nurtures its emotions and mind. Only God, however, can create the child's eternal soul. A soul must have a body on this earth. A body has a soul. Both God and mother are partners in the creation of a baby from the moment of conception.

No privilege is greater than the privilege of creating another human being. And no act requires greater faith!

> EVERY MOTHER HAS THE BREATHTAKING PRIVILEGE OF SHARING WITH GOD IN THE CREATION OF NEW LIFE. SHE HELPS BRING INTO EXISTENCE A SOUL THAT WILL ENDURE FOR ALL ETERNITY.
>
> JAMES KELLER

It was you who formed my inward parts;
you knit me together in my mother's womb.

PSALM 139:13 NRSV

A HIGHER PLAN

Sarah's second child was born with a clubfoot, just as her first child had been. At that time, such a child was called a "child of the devil." But that wasn't true in Sarah's thinking. When she saw that her son had a quick mind, she worked night and day for many years as a maid in other people's homes to pay for his education. She taught her son Thad to keep on fighting, no matter how great the odds against him, and she loved him with all her heart.

When young Thad was cruelly taunted as a "cripple" by his classmates, Sarah comforted and encouraged him, and with each passing year, he became more confident. Thaddeus eventually went to law school. His interest turned to those he saw as less fortunate than himself, especially black slaves.

He often paid the doctor bills of crippled boys, and he once spent $300 of his savings, intended for law books, to buy the freedom of a black man about to be sold away from his family. Over the years, Thaddeus Stevens became loved by black Americans as a hero second only to Abraham Lincoln, and he was considered the greatest defender of former slaves.

A mother's love truly can redeem a child's weakness and turn it into a strength!

> THE MOTHER'S LOVE IS LIKE GOD'S LOVE; HE LOVES US NOT BECAUSE WE ARE LOVABLE, BUT BECAUSE IT IS HIS NATURE TO LOVE, AND BECAUSE WE ARE HIS CHILDREN.
>
> EARL RINEY

IN THIS IS LOVE, NOT THAT WE LOVED GOD BUT THAT HE LOVED US AND SENT HIS SON TO BE THE ATONING SACRIFICE FOR OUR SINS. BELOVED, SINCE GOD LOVED US SO MUCH, WE ALSO OUGHT TO LOVE ONE ANOTHER.

1 JOHN 4:10, 11 NRSV

WISE WORDS

I know the plans I have for you," declares the LORD, "plans to prosper you and not to harm you, plans to give you hope and a future. Then you will call upon me and come and pray to me, and I will listen to you. You will seek me and find me when you seek me with all your heart. I will be found by you."

JEREMIAH 29:11-14

booklist

read more about it...learning

Researchers, teachers, and parents have discovered that not every child takes in information in the same way. So much of a child's success in school is dependent upon identifying learning disabilities and differences and knowing how to help children learn successfully.

- *Active Learning for Children with Disabilities* by Pamela Bailey

- *The Way They Learn* by Cynthia Ulrich Tobias

- *Myth of Laziness: America's Top Learning Expert Shows How Children and Their Parents Can Become More Productive* by Mel Levine, M.D.

- *Forget-Me-Not Bible Story Activities: Making the Bible Unforgettable for Children of All Learning Styles* by Christine Yount

BEAUTY OF PATIENT TEACHING

IN HER BOOK, *AMERICAN Girl,* Mary Cantwell tells of her great embarrassment and agony at not being able to do math like the other children in her class at school. She writes: "It was agony to me to be so stupid. The more Miss Fritzi tried to show me how to translate the marks into symbols, the more cotton seemed to be stuffing the corners of my head. The cotton seemed even thicker on the nights Papa sat beside me at the desk in the living room, pencil points breaking under his fierce attack. I snuffled and shook and his voice took on a steel edge, and when at last my mother shyly volunteered, the suffering eyes we turned on her were identical.

As parents, we never stand so tall as when we stoop to help our children.

"For several nights she sat at the desk . . . and summoned up her old schoolteacher's skills. Sniffling at her left, I bent over a scratch pad watching while her small, shapely hand (a hand that could trace a line of gold leaf as fine as a hair) traced swoops and curlicues. Suddenly they assembled themselves into sense and the cotton fled my head, leaving it as clear and clean as a tide-rinsed seashell. . . . I knew a triumph second only to that I'd known on the morning I finally succeeded in tying my shoelaces into bows. I could add!"

Taking the time to help your child—no matter what the task—can change their world and yours.

Be humble, thinking of others as better than yourself. Don't just think about your own affairs, but be interested in others, too, and in what they are doing. Your attitude should be the kind that was shown us by Jesus Christ.

PHILIPPIANS 2:3-5 TLB

PATIENT LOVE

The daughter of missionaries to India, Wendy resented being put into a "box," and, as a teenager in boarding school, she rebelled against what was expected of her. Her parents returned to Canada so the family might be together, but Wendy continued to rebel. Her mother and father, however, didn't judge or condemn her. She says, "They just kept on loving me. I discovered that I could fight rules and people who criticized me, but I couldn't put up walls against love. Because of my parents' patient love for me, I stopped rebelling, and . . . I recommitted my life to Christ."

> **Children** have more need of models than of critics.
>
> JOSEPH JOUBERT

As a young adult, Wendy is now a missionary to India! One of her students, Anne, had a very negative attitude toward Christianity. Wendy said, "I prayed diligently for Anne, and decided that I would treat her with the same loving-kindness with which my parents had treated me. I accepted Anne as she was, without placing spiritual expectations on her. When Anne realized that I didn't intend to judge her . . . she began opening up to me." In March, Anne accepted Christ into her life. Wendy concludes, "A 'close family' has little to do with geography and being together physically. But [it] has everything to do with loving . . . supporting . . . and communicating with each other."

Be their ideal; let them follow the way you teach and live; be a pattern for them in your love, your faith, and your clean thoughts.

1 TIMOTHY 4:12 TLB

☑ JUST DO IT

Think of one woman in your life who is closed off toward God because of life circumstances or background. It may be:

- A teenager forging independence
- A friend who's experienced loss through death or divorce
- A woman who's perhaps had a negative experience with church.

Then pray this prayer for them every day:

Dear Lord, I thank You for this person You've brought into my life. I pray that You will work in her life, by Your Spirit, through the circumstances and people in her life. I ask that she would come to know You as the Savior and hope of her life. I make myself available to You, if I can be of any use toward this end. And reveal to me my own rebellion toward You, in ways that are great and small, and help me to become more like Christ. Amen.

Consider it all JOY, my brethren, when you encounter various trials.

JAMES 1:2 NASB

THE RIGHT INSPIRATION

When Eleanor Sass was a child, she was hospitalized for appendicitis. Her roommate was a young girl named Mollie, who was injured when an automobile hit the bicycle she was riding. Mollie's legs had been badly broken, and, though the doctors performed several surgeries, Mollie faced a strong possibility that she would never walk again. She became depressed, uncooperative, and cried a great deal. She only seemed to perk up when the morning mail arrived. Most of her gifts were books, games, stuffed animals—all appropriate gifts for a bedridden child.

Then one day a different sort of gift came, this one from an aunt far away. When Mollie tore open the package, she found a pair of shiny, black, patent-leather shoes. The nurses in the room mumbled something about "people who don't use their heads," but Mollie didn't seem to hear them. She was too busy putting her hands in the shoes and "walking" them up and down her blanket. From that day, her attitude changed. She began cooperating with the nursing staff and soon she was in therapy. One day Eleanor heard that her friend had left the hospital—and the best news of all, she had walked out, wearing her shiny new shoes!

Who's Who:

Canaanite Mother

The story of the Canaanite woman told in Matthew 15 presents a striking example of one mother's great faith. Jesus had withdrawn from His teaching when this woman approached Him. She said, "Lord, Son of David, have mercy on me! My daughter is suffering terribly from demon possession." We aren't told why, but Jesus did not answer her. Yet the woman continued to cry out to Him. His disciples, apparently annoyed, urged Jesus to send her away. The woman persisted and knelt down before Him. Their exchange is recounted in Matthew 15:26-29.

She said, "Lord, help me!"

He replied, "It is not right to take the children's bread and toss it to their dogs."

"Yes, Lord," she said, "but even the dogs eat the crumbs that fall from their master's table."

Then Jesus answered, "Woman, you have great faith! Your request is granted." And her daughter was healed from that very hour.

This woman's story provides an ideal model for all who pray. She acknowledged who Christ is, she was persistent, she humbled herself before the Lord, and she prayed with absolute belief in the power of God to heal.

HOLDING HOPE

WAVIE INTENDED ONLY TO skip a day of school, but friendly strangers offered her a ride, and with each mile she traveled, the more difficult it became for her to turn around. Her parents, thinking she had been abducted, almost immediately began to search for her. Several times they thought they were close to finding her, only to have their hopes dashed. Still, they never quit praying for their daughter. They prayed that God would send their love to Wavie and that He would protect her. And they never quit believing that each ring of the phone, each delivery of the mail, might bring word that their daughter was safe and well.

One day Wavie did return. She told of writing hundreds of letters to her parents, ones never mailed. Still, one of her tear-stained messages did come home with her. She had written, in part: "I love and miss you more than I could ever explain. I'm ashamed of what I've done. I pray every night that God will send you my love and take care of you so that one day I'll see all of you again."

Throughout the time she was away, Wavie's prayer for her parents had been nearly identical to that of her parents' prayer for her!

> **There is no** greater love than the love that holds on where there seems nothing left to hold on to.
>
> G.W.C. THOMAS

Love never fails [never fades out or becomes obsolete or comes to an end].

1 CORINTHIANS 13:8 AMP

new insights into ageless questions

I know I should pray about things. But what's the point? Why should we pray to a God who already knows what is going to happen?

Prayer is more than imparting information to God. It is an exercise and one that is primarily for your sake. God knows that you need to verbalize your requests. How else will you know when He's answered you? How will you understand that God is more than a big genie in the sky?

On God's part, it provides a stimulus for interaction. When you go to Him in prayer, He is able to communicate His personal love and appreciation for you. It provides an opportunity for you to experience being in His presence.

Think about your relationship with your own children. Don't you love spending time with them, listening to them, looking for ways to help them and bless them and express your love for them? God has the same feelings for you.

GOD FIRST

> YOU CAN DO EVERYTHING ELSE **RIGHT** AS A PARENT, BUT IF YOU DON'T BEGIN WITH **LOVING GOD,** YOU'RE GOING TO **FAIL.**
>
> ALVIN VANDER GRIEND

SARAH EDWARDS, wife of revivalist and theologian Jonathan Edwards, bore eleven children. At her death, Samuel Hopkins eulogized her in this way:

"She had an excellent way of governing her children. She knew how to make them regard and obey her cheerfully, without loud, angry words, much less heavy blows. . . . If any correction was necessary, she did not administer it in a passion. . . .

"In her directions in matters of importance, she would address herself to the reason of her children, that they might not only know her will, but at the same time be convinced of the reasonableness of it. . . . Her system of discipline was begun at a very early age, and it was her rule to resist the first as well as every subsequent exhibition of temper or disobedience in the child . . . wisely reflecting that until a child will obey their parents, they can never be taught to obey God."

At the close of each day, after all in the family were in bed, Sarah and her husband shared a devotional time together in his study. With eleven children to "tuck into bed," Sarah did not allow any of them leeway in keeping her from this cherished time with her husband!

The LORD our God, the LORD is one.
Love the LORD your God with all your heart and
with all your soul and with all your strength.

DEUTERONOMY 6:4-5

TOP **10** TIPS for Successful Living with a House Full of Kids

1. GIVE THE OLDER CHILDREN JOBS TO DO, AND EXPECT THAT THEY'LL DO THEM.

2. GET REINFORCEMENT FROM YOUR HUSBAND, IF YOU'RE IN A TWO-PARENT HOUSEHOLD.

3. REFRAIN FROM GIVING OLDER CHILDREN THE ACTUAL RESPONSIBILITY OF PARENTING. CHILDREN NEED MOTHERING FROM THEIR MOTHER.

4. GET RID OF CLUTTER, AND MAKE YOUR SPACE AS FRIENDLY AS POSSIBLE.

5. PLAN MEALS AHEAD OF TIME, AND DON'T LET DISHES SIT, WHEN POSSIBLE.

6. SET BOUNDARIES, PARTICULARLY FOR BEDTIME.

7. DON'T OVER-SCHEDULE ACTIVITIES FOR YOUR CHILDREN.

8. REMEMBER, LAUNDRY IS EASIER TO KEEP UP WITH WHEN DONE DAILY. AND DON'T OVERLOOK THE FACT THAT YOUR CHILDREN CAN BE A BIG HELP.

9. SHOW YOUR CHILDREN THAT YOUR MARRIAGE RELATIONSHIP IS A PRIORITY.

10. PUT YOUR RELATIONSHIP WITH GOD FIRST, AND MAKE HIS WORD A PART OF YOUR LIVES.

CONSIDER THIS!

The Psalmist says, "Since my youth, O God, You have taught me, and to this day I declare Your marvelous deeds" (Psalm 71:17). It is easy to look at the simplicity with which children approach life and believe that they are too young to be spoken to or used by God. Scripture makes it clear that children have the ability to receive the message of Christ more readily than adults because their faith has not become clouded by adult skepticism and doubt.

Adults can learn a thing or two about faith and position by observing a child. Jesus says, "I tell you the truth, unless you change and become like little children, you will never enter the kingdom of heaven. Therefore, whoever humbles himself like this child is the greatest in the kingdom of heaven" (Matthew 18:3-4).

Teach your child the simple truths about God, and learn to approach God with the simplicity you see in your child.

A READY HEART

A little girl, only three years old, had just learned she was adopted, but she had failed to react one way or the other to that news. Her mother was at a loss as to how to explain the adoption any further.

The next day at church the little girl watched as a number of people went forward at the close of the service to accept Jesus Christ as their Savior and Lord. She asked her mother, "What are they doing?" Her mother was quick to reply. "God has offered to adopt all of them as His children, and they are taking Him up on His offer so they can live with Him forever in Heaven and always know that He loves

> I THINK THAT SAVING A LITTLE CHILD AND BRINGING HIM TO HIS OWN, IS A DERNED SIGHT BETTER BUSINESS THAN LOAFING AROUND THE THRONE.
>
> JOHN HAY

them with all His heart." The little girl nodded and watched in awe as the pastor prayed with each person.

The next day, the mother overheard her little girl speak into her cocker spaniel's silky ear, "I just wanted you to know I'm 'dopting you 'cause God and Mommy and Daddy have 'dopted me. And that way we can live together forever."

Never assume that a child is too young to follow Christ. As much as a child is able, let them accept and follow. Give approval and full acceptance to their decision. Eventually, "following" will seem to be the only desirable choice for the child to make!

The **fruit** of the **righteous** is a tree of life; and he that winneth souls is wise.

PROVERBS 11:30 KJV

ACTIONS SPEAK LOUDER THAN WORDS

Mary Dow Brine's "Somebody's Mother"—here abbreviated—is a classic worthy to be memorized:

She stood at the crossing and waited long,
Alone, uncared for, amid the throng.
Past the woman so old and gray
Hastened the children on their way.
No one offered a helping hand to her—
So meek, so timid, afraid to stir
Lest the carriage wheels or the horses' feet
Should crowd her down in the slippery street.
He paused beside her and whispered low,
"I'll help you cross, if you wish to go."
Her aged hand on his strong young arm
She placed, and so, without hurt or harm,
He guided the trembling feet along,
Proud that his own were firm and strong.
Then back again to his friends he went,
His young heart happy and well content.
"She's somebody's mother, boys, you know.
For all she's aged and poor and slow.
And I hope some fellow will lend a hand
To help my mother, you understand,
If ever she's poor and old and gray,
When her own dear boy is far away."

This boy's parents taught him not only to be kind, appreciative, and pleasant to his own family and friends but to even see a stranger as someone special.

> **If it is** desirable that children be kind, appreciative, and pleasant, those qualities should be taught—not hoped for.
>
> JAMES DOBSON

THE COMMANDMENT IS A LAMP; AND THE LAW IS LIGHT; AND REPROOFS OF INSTRUCTION ARE THE WAY OF LIFE.

PROVERBS 6:23 KJV

WISE WORDS

Now this is the commandment—the statutes and the ordinances—that the LORD your God charged me to teach you to observe in the land that you are about to cross into and occupy, so that you and your children and your children's children, may fear the LORD your God all the days of your life, and keep all his decrees and his commandments that I am commanding you, so that your days may be long.

DEUTERONOMY 6:1-2 NRSV

booklist

read more about it...adoption

- *Raising Adopted Children, Revised Edition: Practical Reassuring Advice for Every Adoptive Parent*
  by Lois Ruskai Melina

- *Twenty Things Adopted Kids Wish Their Adoptive Parents Knew*
  by Sherrie Eldridge

- *Talk About Adoption*
  by Carrie Kitze

- *Keys to Parenting an Adopted Child*
  by Kathy Lancaster

- *Be My Baby: Parents and Children Talk About Adoption*
  by Gail Kinn

- *Adopting Older Children*
  by Grace Robinson

THE TRUTH ABOUT MOTHERING

A THIRTEEN-YEAR-OLD girl named Amy was not only struggling with growing into womanhood, but also with discovering her identity. She had been adopted from South Korea and had no information about or remembrance of her birth mother. As much as she loved her adoptive parents, she began to speak frequently about what her "real mother" might be like.

During this time, Amy's dentist determined that Amy needed braces. On the day her braces were fitted, Amy went home from the dentist's office in pain. As the day wore on, her discomfort grew, and by bedtime she was miserable. Her mother gave her medication and then invited her to snuggle up in her lap in the rocking chair, just as she had done when she was a little girl. As the mother rocked and stroked Amy, she began to relax in comfort. She was nearly asleep when she said to her mother in a drowsy voice, "I know who my real mom is."

"You do?" her mother asked gently.

"Yes," she replied. "She's the one who takes away the hurting."

Mothers may not always be able to "kiss it and make it well," but the love they give their children goes a long way toward making their children whole.

> A mother . . .
> fills a place so great that there isn't an angel in heaven who wouldn't be glad to give a bushel of diamonds to come down here and take her place.
>
> BILLY SUNDAY

The angel came in unto her, and said, Hail, thou that art highly favoured, the Lord is with thee: blessed art thou among women.

LUKE 1:28 KJV

"Encouragement is the art of "TURNING YOUR CHILDREN ON," helping them to do for themselves, not doing for them."

DR. WILLIAM MITCHELL AND
DR. CHARLES PAUL CONN

TO CORRECT IS TO LOVE

Once upon a time there was a little boy who was given everything he wanted. As an infant, he was given a bottle at the first little whimper. He was picked up and held whenever he fussed. His parents said, "He'll think we don't love him if we let him cry."

He was never disciplined for leaving the yard, even after being told not to. He suffered no consequence for breaking windows or tearing up flower beds. His parents said, "He'll think we don't love him if we stifle his will."

His mother picked up after him, made his bed, and cleaned up all his messes. His parents said, "He'll think we don't love him if we give him chores."

Nobody ever stopped him from using bad words or telling dirty jokes. He was never reprimanded for scribbling on his bedroom wall. His parents said, "He'll think we don't love him if we stifle his creativity."

He never was required to go to Sunday school. His parents said, "He'll think we don't love him if we force religion down his throat."

One day the parents received news that their son was in jail on a felony charge. They cried to each other, "All we ever did was love him and do for him." Unfortunately, that is, indeed, all they did.

Who's Who:

Eli was an Israelite high priest—called by God and descended from a line of priests. The great prophet Samuel served under Eli in the temple from the time Samuel was a very young child. But Eli had one huge thorn in his side: his own sons. Scripture says, in 1 Samuel 2:12, "Eli's sons were wicked men; they had no regard for the LORD." These sons, Hophni and Phinehas, dishonored their father by degrading the sacrifices that were offered to God and by sleeping with the women who, the Bible says, served at the entrance to the Tent of Meeting.

Eli heard of his son's exploits and said, "Why do you do such things? I hear from all the people about these wicked deeds of yours. No, my sons; it is not a good report that I hear." It was the sincere cry of a desperate father. But it was too late. Eli had waited too long to tend to his own children—to instruct, discipline, and encourage them. Now, as adults, they refused to listen.

Eli was a high priest, but a weak father, and this became the ruin of him and his family line. God allowed both of Eli's sons to be killed in battle with the Philistines. When Eli learned of their deaths, and that the Philistines had stolen the Ark of the Covenant, Eli died. When parents correct their children, they show respect for themselves, their children, and most importantly, God. Don't wait too long.

WHAT CAN YOU DO?

DURING A DINNER PARTY, the hosts' two young children entered the dining room totally nude and began to walk slowly on tiptoe around the table. The parents were at first so astonished, and then so embarrassed, that they pretended nothing unusual was happening. They kept the conversation going, and the guests cooperated in the charade, also pretending as if nothing extraordinary was happening in the room.

After completely encircling the table, the children tiptoed from the room. There was a moment of silence at the table as everyone exhaled, and stifled their giggles. Then one of the children was overheard saying to the other in the adjacent hallway, "You see, Mommy was right. It is vanishing cream!"

While their rambunctious energy and inexhaustible curiosity can be tiring to adults, toddlers don't mean to misbehave nearly as much as they mean to make sense of the world in which they find themselves. Your discipline, patience, and encouragement are like red, yellow, and green lights governing their "tear" through the exploration process.

When your children try your patience, try to respond in such a way that you can hear a verdict of "not guilty."

lighten up

A weary teacher had almost completed the week's discussion of the Ten Commandments, when she asked: "Does anyone know what the last commandment is?"

She was surprised to see one of the little girl's hands shoot into the air. "I know, I know, " she said. Then after a dramatic pause to ensure that everyone was listening, the little girl announced, "Thou shalt not uncover thy neighbor's wife!"

BEFORE CHILDREN: I was thankful for material objects like custom furniture, a nice car, and trendy clothes.
AFTER CHILDREN: I'm thankful when the baby spits up and misses my good shoes.

The LORD is on my side; I will not fear:

> " A woman who can cope with
> the terrible twos
> can cope with anything. "
>
> JUDITH CLABES

what can man do unto me? PSALM 118:6 KJV

HOW Do YOU MEASURE Up?

You've heard of IQ and EQ, but what's your SHQ (sense of humor quotient)? Take this little quiz to see where you fall on the scale.

1. When I trip on apparently nothing while walking through a crowded room, do I:
   A. Try to act cool, like nothing's happened?
   B. Get angry and look around for someone to point a finger at?
   C. Give a little chuckle and move on?

2. When someone else falls down (and isn't seriously hurt), do I:
   A. Look away quickly, like I didn't see it?
   B. Think, "Thank heavens it wasn't me?"
   C. Laugh? It's funny when people fall down?

3. When a Three Stooges episode is on, do I:
   A. Give an indignant "hmmmf," and leave the room?
   B. Ask the male in the armchair, "How can you watch this stuff?"
   C. Laugh, either at the three goofballs or at the goofball who thinks they're funnier than anything else in life?

4. When Murphy's Law is the rule of my day, do I:
   A. Despair because I'm not perfect?
   B. Get angry and look to place blame?
   C. Laugh and ask myself, "Okay, now what?"

Score 1 for A; 2 for B; 3 for C. If you scored 10-12, you're doing okay. The tough stuff of life won't get you down. If you scored 7-9, you've got a bit of loosening up to do. If you scored 7 or below, take a day at the spa to relax and then go on a quest for levity. God gave us humor as a supreme coping mechanism and a means of pure enjoyment and connection with others. Lighten up every chance you get.

LAST LAUGH

> ## A GOOD LAUGH IS SUNSHINE IN A HOUSE.
>
> THACKERAY

Business consultant C. W. Metcalf tells how he once signed up for a hospice training program to work with terminally ill patients. He was assigned to Roy, an elderly man with colon cancer. Offering to assist Roy one day, Metcalf said, "Maybe you want me to help you out of those Mickey Mouse pajamas and into something more respectable." Roy whispered back, even in his great pain, "I like these pj's. Mickey reminds me that I can still laugh a little, which is more than the doctor has ever done. Maybe you should get some pj's with Goofy on them." Roy laughed, but Metcalf didn't. "Young man," he continued, "you're one of the most depressing people I've ever met. I'm sure you're a nice person, but if you're here to help, it ain't working." Metcalf was angered to hear the truth put so bluntly.

On the last day of his training, Metcalf learned that Roy had died. His instructor handed him a paper bag that Roy had left for him. Inside, he found a T-shirt with the grinning face of Goofy. A note read: "Put on this shirt at the first sign you're taking yourself too seriously. In other words, wear it all the time." Metcalf laughed! Roy had taught him one of the best lessons he ever learned: humor isn't an occasional joke. It's a basic survival tool for living life to the fullest!

The **light** in the eyes [of him whose heart is joyful] rejoices the **hearts** of others.

PROVERBS 15:30 AMP

MIRACLE OF LIFE

> A **BABY** IS GOD'S **OPINION** THAT THE **WORLD** SHOULD GO ON.
>
> CARL SANDBURG

WHEN ANCIENT men and women witnessed great manifestations of nature's power—such as volcanic eruptions, giant waterfalls, hurricanes, great earthquakes, lightning bolts—they referred to them as "God's deeds," because they knew that no matter how strong they might be as individual people or collective bands of people, they could not do anything as powerful. Even today, great natural catastrophes are termed by insurance companies as "acts of God."

Unfortunately, these displays of nature were often devastating to people, and thus "deeds of God" became equated in the minds of many as "punishments by God." The thinking developed that when God intervenes in the affairs of mankind, it is generally for the purpose of reprimand.

How unfair to God! The truth is, when God chooses to intervene in the affairs of men and to set history on a new course, He does not send a lightning bolt, tidal wave, or tornado—rather, He causes a baby to be born.

The conception of a baby may not be regarded as earthshaking news to anyone other than the baby's family, but from God's perspective, it is the most powerful "deed" He performs!

God blessed them, and God said unto them, be fruitful, and multiply, and replenish the earth, and subdue it.

GENESIS 1:28 KJV

TOP **10** TIPS

for Beating Money Stress
While Bringing Up Baby

Babies are miraculous—and the amount of money it takes to provide for them through age 17 is astounding. Don't let money stress keep you from enjoying your children. Here are some tips that can help you make the most of your money and your child-rearing years.

1. DECIDE NOT MOVE INTO A BIGGER HOME.

2. MAKE YOUR HOME AS ENERGY EFFICIENT AS POSSIBLE.

3. CONSIDER RAISING YOUR FAMILY IN AN AREA WHERE HOUSING PRICES AND TAXES ARE EASIER TO MANAGE.

4. THINK ABOUT A HOME OFFICE, WHICH ALLOWS TAX DEDUCTIONS.

5. SET STRICT LIMITS ON DISCRETIONARY INCOME, ESPECIALLY WHEN EATING OUT IS CONCERNED.

6. BUY FOOD WHOLESALE.

7. AVOID BUYING A NEW CAR. USE THE INTERNET OR AUCTIONS.

8. TWO WORDS: SECOND-HAND. CLOTHES. BEDDING. FURNITURE. HOME DÉCOR. SPORTING EQUIPMENT.

9. HAVE CHILDREN SAVE UP AND PAY FOR DESIGNER CLOTHES OR OTHER SPECIAL ITEMS THEY WANT.

10. REMEMBER THAT GOD WILL PROVIDE FOR YOUR NEEDS. TRUST HIM, AND DON'T LET STRESS ABOUT MONEY GET THE BEST OF YOUR LIFE.

CONSIDER THIS!

All mothers, especially those who tend to be intro-
verted, need downtime to unwind. The same is true
for babies and small children. Some parents would-
n't consider putting their child in their room for a
time, with books or toys, to have some quiet
because they feel a sense of guilt. In fact, this "quiet
time" can be a much-needed break for children and
parents, and it can establish a life-long attitude in a
child that time alone is not only okay, but healthy
and beneficial.

When Christ was ministering on earth, He took
time away to rest and spend communing with God
the Father. Rest and quiet is an innate need for
human beings. In our culture so bent toward constant activity, it is valuable to instill the importance
of quiet and solitude in your child early in life.

QUIET TIME

A mother was at her wit's end. Her baby had screamed all day, nonstop. She knew he was in the throes of teething, but what could she do? She had tried rocking him, giving him pieces of ice, carrying him, and every other remedy suggested by her mother and friends. Nothing had worked. Finally, in great frustration, she laid her child in his crib, took a shower, washed her hair, set it, and went to sit under her hair dryer. She thought, *If I can't stop my baby's crying, at least I can stop myself from hearing his cries.* To her surprise, when she came out from under the hair dryer to get a drink of water, she found her baby asleep.

> **REMEMBER, WHEN YOUR CHILD HAS A TANTRUM, DON'T HAVE ONE OF YOUR OWN.**
>
> DR. J. KURIANSKY

The next day when he began to cry, she turned on the hair dryer, and within minutes, he was calm. She discovered the vacuum cleaner also had this effect, as well as the sound of the tumbling dryer. She said, "I got more housework done than I ever dreamed possible, all in an attempt to calm my child."

Sometimes tantrums are the result of over-stimulation. A child is too tired, surrounded by too many sights and sounds, feeling too many conflicting feelings, and, yes, even receiving too much reaction from parents! In removing some of the stimulation, a child is given just what he needs: calm.

Everyone who competes in the games goes into strict training. They do it to get a crown that will not last; but we do it to get a crown that will last forever.

1 CORINTHIANS 9:25

WORTH IN CHILDHOOD WONDER

Jane Goodall spent more than thirty years in Africa and became the world's top authority on chimpanzees. She writes about the support that helped her get started: "When I decided that the place for me was Africa, everybody said to my mother, 'Why don't you tell Jane to concentrate on something attainable?' But I have a truly remarkable mother.

"When I was two years old, I took a crowd of earthworms to bed to watch how they wriggled in the bedclothes. How many mothers would have said 'ugh' and thrown them out the window? But mine said, 'Jane, if you leave the worms here they'll be dead in the morning. They need the earth.' So I quickly gathered them up and ran with them into the garden. My mother always looked at things from my point of view."

Seeing things from your child's point of view is one of the most valuable ways to interact with your child. Periodically get down on the floor and play with your child. As you do, show by example how to play, how to share, how to interact, how to cooperate or compete in a friendly manner, and how to put away toys or organize a play space. What you do, your child will do!

> IN PRACTICING THE ART OF PARENTHOOD AN OUNCE OF EXAMPLE IS WORTH A TON OF PREACHMENT.
> WILFERD A. PETERSON

LET YOUR LIGHT SO SHINE BEFORE MEN, THAT THEY MAY SEE YOUR GOOD WORKS, AND GLORIFY YOUR FATHER WHICH IS IN HEAVEN.

MATTHEW 5:16 KJV

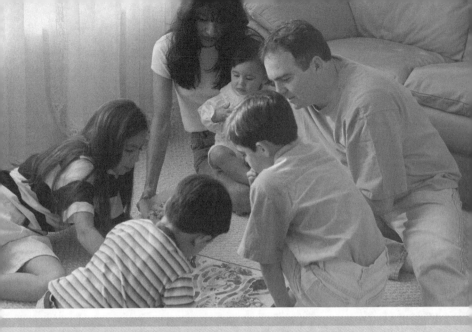

WISE WORDS

O LORD, how manifold are your works! In wisdom you have made them all; the earth is full of your creatures. Yonder is the sea, great and wide, creeping things innumerable are there, living things both small and great. There go the ships, and Leviathan that you formed to sport in it. These all look to you to give them their food in due season; when you give to them, they gather it up; when you open your hand, they are filled with good things.

PSALM 104:24-28 NRSV

booklist

- *It's a Miracle 2: More Inspiring True Stories Based on the PAX TV Series, It's a Miracle*
  by Richard Thomas

- *God Is in the Small Stuff*
  by Bruce Bickel, Stan Jantz

- *The Little Book of Big Dreams: Stories of Success, Triumph & Inspiration*
  by Alan C. Elliott

- *Chicken Soup for the Mother's Soul, 101 Stories to Open the Hearts and Rekindle the Spirits of Mothers*
  by Jack Canfield, Mark Victor Hansen, Marci Shimoff

HEAVEN'S HAND

WHILE DRIVING ALONG a freeway on a cold, rainy night, the adults in the front seat of a car were talking when suddenly, they heard the horrifying sound of a car door opening, then the whistle of wind, and a sickening muffled sound. They quickly turned and saw that the three-year-old child riding in the backseat had fallen out of the car and was tumbling along the freeway. The driver screeched to a stop, and then raced back toward her motionless child. To her surprise, she found all the traffic stopped just feet away from her child. Her daughter had not been hit.

A truck driver offered his assistance and drove the girl to a nearby hospital. The doctors there rushed her into the emergency room, and soon came back with the good news: other than being unconscious and bruised and skinned from her tumble, the girl was fine. No broken bones. No apparent internal damage.

As the mother rushed to her child, the little girl opened her eyes and said, "Mommy, you know I wasn't afraid." The mother asked, "What do you mean?" The little girl explained, "While I was lying on the road waiting for you to get back to me, I looked up and right there I saw Jesus holding back the traffic with His arms out."

> **God has** given you your child, that the sight of him, from time to time, might remind you of His goodness, and induce you to praise Him with filial reverence.
> CHRISTIAN SCRIVER

See how very much our heavenly Father loves us, for he allows us to be called his children— think of it—and we really *are!*

1 JOHN 3:1 TLB

RELINQUISHING

Time magazine ran in its January 25, 1988, issue an article about the introduction of the videocassette recorder in the marketplace. The article said: "The company had made a crucial mistake. While at first Sony kept its Beta technology mostly to itself, JVC, the Japanese inventor of the VHS [format], shared its secret with a raft of other firms. As a result, the market was overwhelmed by the sheer volume of the VHS machines being produced."

The result was a drastic undercutting of Sony's market share of VCRs. The first year, Sony lost forty percent of the market and by 1987, it controlled only ten percent of the market with its Beta format. In the end, Sony jumped on the VHS bandwagon. While it continued for many years to make Beta-format video equipment and tapes, Sony's switch to VHS ultimately sent Beta machines to the consumer-electronics graveyard.

> **I have held** many things in my hands and lost them all; but the things I have placed in God's hands, those I always possess.
> EARLINE STEELBURG

Even in a cutthroat business, sharing has its rewards. How much deeper, broader, and richer are the rewards of sharing those things that are spiritual and eternal in nature.

I know the one in whom I have put my trust, and I am sure that he is able to guard until that day what I have entrusted to him.

2 TIMOTHY 1:12 NRSV

✓ JUST DO IT

to do | urgent

Nearly all followers of Christ have portions of themselves or their lives that they can't or won't relinquish to God. If that statement rings true in your heart, try this. Examine your heart, and make a list of five things you believe you are holding back from God. They might be:

- Anxiety about the future
- A key relationship that you're trying to "fix" on your own
- Your children
- Sin, like jealously or discontent
- Material possessions.

Pray about these things honestly with God, using David's words as your guide:

Search me, O God, and know my heart; test me and know my anxious thoughts. See if there is any offensive way in me, and lead me in the way everlasting (Psalm 139:23-24).

BLESSED COMFORT

A YOUNG GIRL WAS VERY late in coming home from school. Her mother watched the clock nervously and with growing concern. Finally she arrived. Her mother, nearly frantic at that point, hugged her daughter, and after giving her a thorough appraisal and realizing nothing appeared to be wrong, demanded, "Where were you? What took you so long? Haven't I told you to be home by 4 o'clock?"

The girl answered her mother's first question, "I was at Mary's house."

"And what was so important that you couldn't get home on time?" her mother scolded.

Her daughter replied, "Her favorite doll got broken."

> **Who ran to me** when I fell, and would some pretty story tell, or kiss the place to make it well? My mother.
>
> ANN TAYLOR

"Did you break it?" the mother asked. When her daughter shook her head "no," she then asked, "Could the doll be fixed?" Again, the girl replied with a "no." Both bewildered and frustrated, the mother asked a third time, "So what was the point of staying so long?"

Tears began to well up in the little girl's eyes and stream down her face under her mother's inquisition. "I helped her cry," she said softly.

The Scriptures tell us to "rejoice with those that do rejoice, and weep with those that weep" (Romans 12:15). Mothers may not be able to do everything for their children, but they all can do that!

[Thus says the Lord:] "As a mother comforts her child, so I will comfort you."

ISAIAH 66:13 NRSV

|new insights into ageless questions

I try so hard to teach my child to be kind and empathetic, but it doesn't seem to be sinking in. Do you have any words of wisdom for me?

You certainly aren't the only mother struggling with this dilemma. Studies of middle and high school kids reveal a growing lack of empathy toward their peers and people in general. Researchers believe, in part, that this comes from exposure to thousands of depictions of violent acts on TV, in movies, and in video games that has numbed the empathetic tendency in kids.

It is critical that you continue to ensure that your child does not become desensitized to other people's hurt and pain. Monitor what your children watch on TV, what movies they see, and what they're exposed to on the Internet. Open dialogues about current events in the news that depict the suffering of others—from the mother of a child who's been killed and the parents of a child who's committed a crime to the criminals themselves.

You can also introduce ideas of a fallen world and a God who desires that His people aim to live by a higher standard. Pray together for those who are in need. Introduce scripture and environments that promote compassion, such as community or church outreach projects. Perhaps most importantly of all, model empathetic behavior in your relationships. Children live what they see.

TRUE WELCOME HOME

JONI EARECKSON TADA writes a wonderful tribute in *Secret Strength* to a genuine "home, sweet home":

"Not long ago I entered a friend's home and immediately sensed the glory of God. No, that impression was not based on some heebie-jeebie feeling or superspiritual instinct. And it had nothing to do with several Christian plaques I spotted hanging in the hallway. Yet there was a peace and orderliness that pervaded that home. Joy and music hung in the air. Although the kids were normal, active youngsters, everyone's activity seemed to dovetail together, creating the impression that the home had direction, that the kids really cared about each other, that the parents put love into action.

"We didn't even spend that much time 'fellowshipping' in the usual sense of the word—talking about the Bible or praying together. Yet we laughed. And really heard each other. And opened our hearts like family members. After dinner I left that home refreshed. It was a place where God's essential being was on display. His kindness, His love, His justice. It was filled with God's glory."

The sweetness of the Lord makes any home sweet!

lighten up

Signs Seen in Kitchens:

- Ring bell for maid service. If no answer, do it yourself!
- I clean house every other day. Today is the other day.
- If you write in the dust, please don't date it!
- My house was clean last week, too bad you missed it!
- I came, I saw, I decided to order take out.
- It doesn't always look like this: Some days it's even worse.
- A messy kitchen is a happy kitchen, and this kitchen is delirious.
- A balanced diet is a cookie in each hand!
- Thou shalt not weigh more than thy refrigerator.
- Blessed are they who can laugh at themselves for they shall never cease to be amused.
- Countless number of people have eaten in this kitchen and gone on to lead normal lives.

> "None of us lives to himself alone and none of us dies to himself alone. If we live, we live to the Lord; and if we die, we die to the Lord. So, whether we live or die, we belong to the Lord."

ROMANS 14:7-8

for the other, and all live for God. T.J. BACH

BELIEF BEGINS AT HOME

> THE **SCHOOL** WILL TEACH CHILDREN **HOW** TO READ, BUT THE ENVIRONMENT OF THE **HOME** MUST TEACH THEM **WHAT** TO READ. THE **SCHOOL** CAN TEACH THEM HOW TO **THINK**, BUT THE **HOME** MUST TEACH THEM WHAT TO **BELIEVE**.
>
> CHARLES A. WELLS

LEWIS SMEDES OF Fuller Theological Seminary, has written a wonderful tribute to the impact a godly home can have upon a child's faith:

"May I share with you some reasons why I believe? All good reasons, none of them the really real reason. There's my family. I believe because I was brought up in a believing family. I don't make any bones about that. I don't know what would have happened to me if I had been born in the depths of Manchuria of a Chinese family. I just don't know. I do know that I was led to believe in the love of God as soon as I learned I should eat my oatmeal. We did a lot of believing in our house. We didn't have much else to do, as a matter of fact. Other kids sang 'Jesus loves me this I know 'cause the Bible tells me so.' I sang, 'Jesus loves me this I know, 'cause my ma told me so.'

"I wasn't alone. You probably heard about a reporter asking the great German theologian, Karl Barth, toward the end of his career: 'Sir, you've written these great volumes about God, great learned tomes about all the difficult problems of God. How do you know they're all true?' And the great theologian smiled and said, 'Cause my mother said so!'

Families are God's primary missionary society.

Teach a child to choose the right path, and when he is older he will remain upon it.

PROVERBS 22:6 TLB

TOP **10** TIPS — for Bible Readings for Children

1. WHO MADE THE WORLD? (GENESIS 1:1-25)

2. THE WOMAN WHO TRADED HER BEAUTIFUL HOME FOR AN APPLE (GENESIS 3:1-6)

3. A COLORFUL COAT (GENESIS 37:1-34)

4. THE BOY WHO COULD HEAR GOD SPEAK (1 SAMUEL 3:1-21)

5. DAVID AND THE GIANT (1 SAMUEL 17:1-58)

6. THE STAR THAT GAVE DIRECTIONS (MATTHEW 2:1-11)

7. THREE FISH STORIES (JONAH 1:1-17; LUKE 5:4-8; JOHN 21:4-11)

8. MR. SELFISHNESS, MR. CURIOSITY, MR. KIND-HEART (LUKE 10:30-37)

9. THE BOY WHO RAN FROM HOME (LUKE 15:11-24)

10. NINE MEN WHO FORGOT TO SAY THANK YOU (LUKE 17:12-19)

CONSIDER
THIS!

We can learn a great deal by observing how our children approach life. Kids live in the now. They laugh boisterously. They're open to new ways of thinking about things. They observe scrupulously and make brutally honest observations. Faith is also much easier for children. They take things at face value, believe what others tell them.

Jesus said we should emulate children with regard to the ease with which they embrace faith. Consider Jesus' words from this passage: "Let the little children come to me, and do not hinder them, for the kingdom of God belongs to such as these. I tell you the truth, anyone who will not receive the kingdom of God like a little child will never enter it" (Mark 10:14,15). A parent does well to strive for the wisdom of an adult and the heart of a child.

STRAIGHT SHOOTERS

A little girl shouted with glee at the unexpected appearance of her grandmother in her nursery. "I've come to tuck you into bed and give you a goodnight kiss," the grandmother explained. "Will you read me a story first?" the little girl asked. Grandma, dressed elegantly for the impending dinner party downstairs, couldn't resist the soulful plea in her granddaughter's eyes. "All right," she replied, "but just one."

At the close of the story, the little girl snuggled into her bed, ready for sleep, but not before she said, "Thank you, Grandma. You look pretty tonight." The grandmother smiled and replied, "Yes,

LEVEL WITH YOUR CHILD BY BEING HONEST. NOBODY SPOTS A PHONY QUICKER THAN A CHILD.

M. MACCRACKEN

I have to be pretty for the dinner party your parents are hosting."

"I know," the little girl said. "Mommy and Daddy are entertaining some very important people downstairs."

"Why, yes," said the grandmother. "But how did you know that? Was it because I surprised you by coming upstairs tonight? Was it my dress that gave it away?" Each time her granddaughter shook her head with a vigorous "no." Finally, the grandmother asked, "Was it that I only read one story to you?"

"No," the little girl giggled. "Just listen! Mommy is laughing at all of Daddy's jokes."

In all things [be] willing to live honestly.

HEBREWS 13:18 KJV

EOL AT HOME

Two well-bred, blue-blooded dogs were walking primly along the street with their noses held high. They encountered a big scruffy dog who obviously was of the Heinz-57-Varieties pedigree. At first they tried daintily to side-step the friendly alley dog, but they were unable to do so. He was eager to make friends and trotted alongside them. One of the lady dogs said, "We really must go," to which the alley dog replied, "Well, all right, but first tell me your names so I'll know what to call you dames if I see you again."

The purebred replied haughtily, "My name is Miji, spelled M-I-J-I." The other said daintily,

"My name is Miki, spelled M-I-K-I."

"Pleased to meet you," said the low-class dog, and then he added, "My name is Fido—spelled P-H-Y-D-E-A-U-X."

Home should be a place where there's no room for pride. Respect and self-dignity, yes, but haughty arrogance born of position? No! Respect your little ones and serve them. Honor your elders and give your best to them. Don't play favorites in relationships or allow a child to think he is favored. Ultimately, home should be a place marked by "equal-opportunity love."

HOME
IS THE PLACE
WHERE THE
GREAT ARE SMALL
AND THE SMALL
ARE GREAT.

[JESUS SAID,] "MANY THAT ARE FIRST SHALL BE LAST; AND THE LAST SHALL BE FIRST."

MATTHEW 19:30 KJV

WISE WORDS

People were bringing even infants to him that he might touch them; and when the disciples saw it, they sternly ordered them not to do it. But Jesus called for them and said, "Let the little children come to me, and do not stop them; for it is to such as these that the kingdom of God belongs.

LUKE 18:15,16 NRSV

Such ever was love's way; to rise, it stoops.
ROBERT BROWNING

booklist

Many parents who've exhausted conventional approaches to childhood issues have looked into alternative methods of addressing their child's needs. Here are a few books that have helped parents toward that end.

- **Raising the Highly Healthy Child**
  by Walt Larimore, M.D.

- **Alternative Medicine: The Christian Handbook**
  by Donal O'Mathuna, Ph.D. and Walt Larimore, M.D.

- **Hands On Baby Massage**
  by Michelle Kluck-Ebbin

- **Train Up Your Children in the Way They Should Eat**
  by Sharon Broer

- **When Your Child Is Hyperactive**
  by David Hawkins

- **The Bible Cure for ADD and Hyperactivity**
  by Don Colbert, M.D.

NO REST FOR THE WORRIED

KAIS RAYES WRITES THAT he and his wife found their whole life turned upside down when their first child was born. Every night, the baby seemed to be fussy, and many nights, it seemed to the young couple that their baby cried far more than he slept. Says Rayes, "My wife would wake me up, saying, 'Get up, honey! Go see why the baby is crying!'" As a result, Rayes found himself suffering from severe sleep deprivation.

While complaining to his coworkers about his problem one day, one of his colleagues suggested a book on infant massage. He immediately went in search of the book and that night, he tried the technique, gently rubbing his baby's back, arms, head, and legs until the baby was completely relaxed and obviously had fallen into a deep sleep. Quietly tiptoeing from the darkened room so as not to disturb the rhythmic breathing of the baby, he made his way directly to his own bed in hopes of enjoying a well-deserved full night of sleep.

But, in the middle of the night, his wife awoke him in a panic. "Get up, honey!" she said as she jostled him awake. "Go see why the baby is not crying!"

Small boy:

"If I'm noisy they give me a spanking . . . if I'm quiet they take my temperature."

CORONET

Search me, O God, and know my **heart;** try me and know my anxious **thoughts.**

PSALM 139:23 NASB

"A mother is the one who is STILL THERE when everyone else has deserted you."

STEADFAST COMMITMENT

A number of years ago a popular Mother's Day card summed up what many adult women feel. The cover of the card read, "Now that we have a mature, adult relationship, there's something I'd like to tell you." On the inside were these words: "You're still the first person I think of when I fall down and go boom."

None of us ever get beyond feeling a "need" for our mothers—the one person who has nurtured us, comforted us, and cared for us as no other person ever has or ever will. It is only when we are mothers ourselves, however, that we tend to realize how important our own mothers were to us. As Victoria Farnsworth has written:

Not until I became a mother did I
understand how much my
mother had sacrificed for me.

Not until I became a mother
did I feel
how hurt my mother was
when I disobeyed.

Not until I became a mother
did I know

how proud my mother was
when I achieved.

Not until I became a mother
did I realize
how much my mother loves
me.

Why not call your mother today and tell her how much you love her?

Who's Who:

The Shunammite Woman

A well-to-do woman lived in the town of Shunam, and she showed kindness and opened her home to the great prophet Elisha. She even created a room for him, so Elisha would have a permanent place of his own whenever he traveled to the town.

Elisha appreciated her kindness, saying, "You have gone to all this trouble for us. Now what can be done for you? Can we speak on your behalf to the king or the commander of the army?" She could have given many replies—blessing, continued wealth, commendation. Instead she answered this way, "I have a home among my own people." This reply spoke to her character and her contentment with her place in life.

One of the best gifts and qualities you can pass on to your children is to model the effectiveness that comes with being content in who you are, in your place and season in life. The story of Elisha and the Shunammite woman becomes even more interesting. You can find the entire story in 2 Kings, chapter 4.

WHAT TO WEAR!

IN HER BOOK *MURPHY Must Have Been a Mother,* Teresa Bloomingdale tells about her daughter's preparing for high school. "I don't have anything to wear," the daughter complained.

Mother agreed, "I know that, honey, and I told you we'd go on a shopping spree next Saturday."

"I can't buy clothes now!" the daughter said.

"Why not?" asked Mom, "School starts next week."

The daughter said, "I can't get clothes for school until I go to school and see what clothes I should get. What if I showed up in jeans and all the other girls were in skirts? I'd die!"

"Then wear a skirt," the mother suggested.

"And find everyone else in jeans?" the daughter asked. When Mom suggested she call a friend and find out what she was going to wear, the daughter said, "Are you kidding? She'd think I don't have a mind of my own!"

Another friend finally called, and the two girls decided on their first-day-of-the-year outfits: blue jeans, white knit shirts, white bobby sox, and top-sider shoes. The author wrote, "And these are the girls who spent eight years complaining because they had to wear look-alike uniforms!"

> **The only thing** children wear out faster than shoes are parents and teachers.

God gives **power** to the **tired** and worn out, and **strength** to the **weak**.

ISAIAH 40:29 TLB

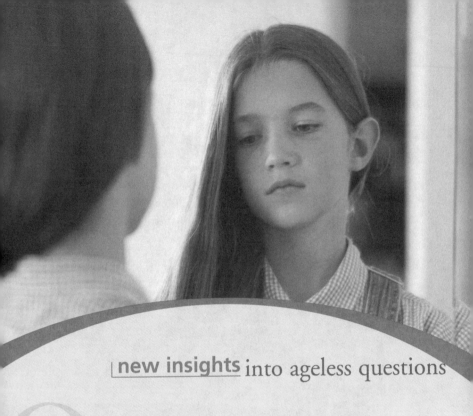

new insights into ageless questions

My preteen daughter is about to drive me mad. She's moody, impatient, and given to extremes. I feel like I can barely speak to her without starting an argument. What's going on?

In *Daughters,* psychiatrist Stella Chess and writer Jane Whitbread write: "Life with a daughter of nine through twelve is a special experience for parents, particularly mothers. In a daughter's looks, actions, attitudes, passions, loves, and hates, in her fears and her foibles, a mother will see herself at the same age. You are far enough away to have some perspective on what your daughter is going through. Still, you are close enough, if reminded, to feel it all again."

The drama, the extremes, the emotional turbulence—the things that make it tough to deal with your adolescent daughter were also part of your experience as an adolescent. Allow that thought to help you gain the perspective you need to walk with your child through this coming of age. Adolescents may begin to say they don't need you and act like they don't want you, but they do—more than ever. And this is a time when you need to lean on your Heavenly Father—more than ever.

Fun Trivia

The Bible is filled with stories of people showing kindness to mere acquaintances or strangers, some who are just passing through.

- Abraham with the Three Visitors (Genesis 18)
- Moses and the Midian Daughters (Exodus 2:17)
- Elisha and the Shunammite woman (2 Kings 4)
- The Good Samaritan (Luke 10:25-37)
- The Philippian Jailer (Acts 16:33)
- The Islanders—not a singing group, but a group of helpful people on the Island of Malta (Acts 28:2)

And that's just to name a few. Kindness toward strangers or acquaintances is kindness for its own sake. A person, such as the Good Samaritan, acts with no regard for reciprocity. This is the approach to kindness and compassion that all believers in Christ should strive toward each day.

REACHING OUT

Kind words can be short
and **easy to speak,** but their
echoes are truly **endless.**

MOTHER TERESA

When the American poet and writer Edgar Guest was a young man, his first child died. He wrote about this experience: "There came a tragic night when our first baby was taken from us. I was lonely and defeated. There didn't seem to be anything in life ahead of me that mattered very much.

"I had to go to my neighbor's drugstore the next morning for something, and he motioned for me to step behind the counter with him. I followed him into his little office at the back of the store. He put both hands on my shoulders and said, 'Eddie, I can't really express what I want to say, the sympathy I have in my heart for you. All I can say is that I'm sorry, and I want you to know that if you need anything at all, come to me. What is mine is yours.'"

Guest recalls that this man was "just a neighbor across the way—a passing acquaintance." He says of the druggist that he "may long since have forgotten that moment when he gave me his hand and his sympathy, but I shall never forget it—never in all my life. To me it stands out like the silhouette of a lonely tree against a crimson sunset."

Is there someone who needs to hear your kind word today?

She opens her mouth in skillful
and godly Wisdom, and on her
tongue is the law of kindness
[giving counsel and instruction.]

EPHESIANS 5:33 AMP

SCHOOL BLUES

A BABY IS AN ANGEL WHOSE WINGS DECREASE AS HIS LEGS INCREASE.

A WOMAN ONCE told this story about her young son who wouldn't go to kindergarten:

"I can't go to school!" he would cry, his big blue eyes filling up with tears. "There's a gorilla up on the corner waiting to gobble me up! You can't see him, but he's there! He hides when grownups come around. Do you want me to be gobbled up by a gorilla?"

By the time the first ten days of school had passed, this mother had tried everything: bribery, pleading, threatening. She even locked him out of the house only to find him sitting under the neighbor's bushes, waiting for the time to come home.

Then one day as he dawdled on the porch steps pleading with his mother not to send him to sure death, one of his classmates, Tommy, came walking up the street and talked him into going to school. Her son met Tommy every day for the rest of the year.

This mother writes, "Wherever you are today, Tommy, know that you have my undying gratitude, though I do have one request. Your kindergarten pal has been in school for eighteen years and is still playing eeny-meeny-miney-mo with his college majors. Would you mind dropping in and cajoling this kid into graduating?"

God will let you laugh again; you'll raise the roof with shouts of joy.

JOB 8:21 MSG

TOP **10** TIPS for Helping Your Kids Adjust to School (and other new situations)

1. AIM TO MAINTAIN ROUTINE AND RITUAL IN YOUR CHILD'S LIFE.

2. PREPARE FOR SAYING GOOD-BYE TO PEOPLE YOUR CHILD MAY HAVE MET IN PRESCHOOL OR OTHER REGULAR PLAY GROUPS.

3. BEGIN TO CULTIVATE A SENSE OF EXCITEMENT ABOUT SCHOOL. TAKE YOUR CHILD TO PLAY ON THE PLAYGROUND DURING OFF-HOURS. DRIVE BY TO POINT OUT RECESS TIMES OR BUSES.

4. START DOING SOME OF THE ACADEMIC ACTIVITIES YOUR CHILD WILL DO IN SCHOOL.

5. REFRAIN FROM MAKING TOO BIG A DEAL OUT OF THE TRANSITION.

6. INTRODUCE YOUR CHILD TO OTHER CHILDREN WHO WILL BE IN THEIR CLASS, IF POSSIBLE.

7. MAKE A BIG DEAL OF GETTING A NEW "SCHOOL BACKPACK," SUPPLIES, NEW SHOES . . .

8. USE BOOKS AND VIDEOS THAT INTRODUCE SCHOOL AND LEARNING IN A POSITIVE LIGHT.

9. PRAY FOR YOUR CHILD AND WITH YOUR CHILD ABOUT THE UPCOMING CHANGE.

10. REMIND YOUR CHILD (AND YOURSELF!) THAT GOD IS WITH THEM WHEREVER THEY GO.

CONSIDER THIS!

How difficult is it to show kindness toward others? True kindness isn't simply a good act. It is a word or action that flows naturally from a humble heart, a spirit that is selfless, a mind that isn't concerned with how others will respond. True kindness comes as a natural response to God's expansive loving-kindness toward His children. This is why Peter writes, "His divine power has given us everything we need for life and godliness through our knowledge of him who called us by his own glory and goodness. For this very reason, make every effort to add to your faith goodness; and to goodness, knowledge; and to knowledge, self-control; and to self-control, perseverance; and to perseverance, godliness; and to godliness, brotherly kindness; and to brotherly kindness, love" (2 Peter 1:3,5-7).

Seek a life where kindness and brotherly love are natural extensions of the inward response to God's love and grace toward His children.

EFFECTS OF KINDNESS

A little girl once paid a visit to relatives who lived in the country. While walking along a country road, she found a land terrapin also walking on the warmed pavement. As she moved closer to examine it, the terrapin closed its shell like a vice. When she tried to pry him open with a stick, her uncle intervened, "No, no. That is not the way. I'll show you what we need to do."

The uncle picked up the small creature and carried it into the house. There he set it on the hearth. In a few minutes the terrapin began to get warm; he stuck out his head and feet, and calmly crawled toward the girl.

"People are sort of like terrapins too," her uncle said. "If you try to force people to do anything, they'll usually close up tightly. But if you warm them up with a little kindness, they'll more than likely open up and come your way."

If you had to pick only one trait around which to live all the time, what would it be? Order, honors, knowledge, passion, fame? Probably not. The most livable of all traits is one every person can show: kindness.

> IT IS BETTER TO KEEP CHILDREN TO THEIR DUTY BY A SENSE OF HONOR AND BY KINDNESS THAN BY FEAR.
>
> TERENCE

Do not irritate and provoke your children
to anger [do not exasperate them to
resentment] but rear them [tenderly] in
the training and discipline and the counsel
and admonition of the Lord.

EPHESIANS 6:4 AMP

WELCOMING

Corrie ten Boom's character was shaped to a great extent by the people who visited in her home. Her mother, a gentle and compassionate woman, was able to bring harmony even to cramped quarters filled with divergent personalities. She loved guests and had a gift for "stretching a guilder until it cried." Those who came to their home found music, fun, food, and interesting conversations. Corrie kept a "blessing box" to collect coins for missionary projects, and she always gave guests an opportunity to be a blessing, even as they were blessed by the ten Boom hospitality. The soup may have been watered down, but the oval table always had room for unexpected guests who arrived just before mealtime. The atmosphere was one of gezellig, of warm exuding friendship, and it wove its way into the very fabric of Corrie's personality.

In later years as Corrie ten Boom traveled the world and was dependent upon the invitations of other Christians, she seldom stayed in hotels. Instead, she graciously accepted food and lodging from others. She once said, "I think that I am enjoying the reward for the wide open doors and hearts of our home." To those she visited, however, she was now the angel unaware, bringing with her welcome gezellig.

> WHEN HOME IS RULED ACCORDING TO GOD'S WORD, ANGELS MIGHT BE ASKED TO STAY WITH US, AND THEY WOULD NOT FIND THEMSELVES OUT OF THEIR ELEMENT.
>
> C.H. SPURGEON

I WILL MEDITATE ON YOUR PRECEPTS, AND CONTEMPLATE YOUR WAYS. I WILL DELIGHT MYSELF IN YOUR STATUTES; I WILL NOT FORGET YOUR WORD.

PSALM 119:15,16 NKJV

WISE WORDS

Above all, maintain constant love for one another, for love covers a multitude of sins. Be hospitable to one another without complaining. Like good stewards of the manifold grace of God, serve one another with whatever gift each of you has received. Whoever speaks must do so as one speaking the very words of God; whoever serves must do so with the strength that God supplies, so that God may be glorified in all things through Jesus Christ. To him belong the glory and the power forever and ever. Amen.

1 PETER 4:8-11 NRSV

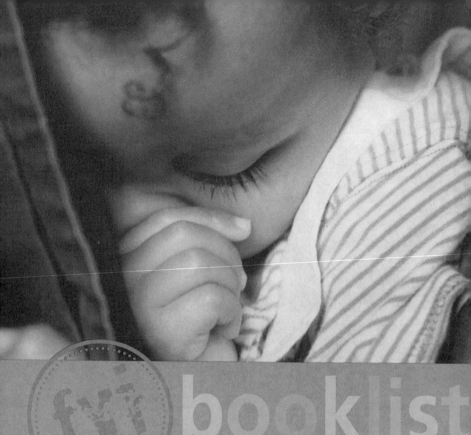

booklist

read more about it...sleep

The number one factor leading to depression of new moms is lack of sleep. Here are some of the most popular and useful guides for new parents who are trying to get their precious little ones to sleep through the night.

- *Healthy Sleep Habits, Happy Child*
  by Marc Weissbluth

- *Solve Your Child's Sleep Problems*
  by Richard Feber

- *The Happiest Baby on the Block*
  by Harvey Karp

- *Nighttime Parenting: How to Get Your Baby and Child to Sleep*
  by William Sears, M.D.

- *In Search of Sleep: Straight Talk About Babies, Toddlers and Night Waking*
  by Bonny Reichert

SLEEP DEPRIVATION

IN *MURPHY MUST HAVE Been a Mother,* Teresa Bloomingdale recalls a conversation she had with her husband, who said, "I love new babies."

"Since when?" I joked. "You were the one who always wished they could be born housebroken and able to play baseball! You had no patience at all with the squalling infants who leaked from both ends and spit up on every shirt you owned. It wasn't until they got into their terrible twos that you thought the kids were worth keeping!"

"That's not true, and you know it," he said with a sigh. "I truly loved those infants, even the ones who couldn't tell time and kept us up all night. . . . Don't tell me you wouldn't just love to start all over again!"

"True, I loved having a new baby every year . . . when I was young and lively and had not yet become addicted to sleep. But at our age? No, thank you."

In planning to help her son and daughter-in-law, Bloomingdale was determined to be the model grandmother—up at night, folding diapers, making formula. But then she discovered she was out of a job. The baby's great-grandmother had arrived to help out!

Is it true that the elderly need less sleep? If so, great-grandmas truly may be best suited for newborns!

> **Insomnia:** a contagious disease often transmitted from babies to parents.
>
> SHANNON FIFE

There is a **right time** for everything: A time to be born.

ECCLESIASTES 3:1,2 TLB

POWERFUL PRAYER

The great preacher Billy Sunday told the story of a minister who was making calls one day. He came to one home, and, when a child answered the door, he asked for her mother. She replied, "You cannot see Mother, for she prays from nine to ten." The minister waited forty minutes. When the woman finally came out of her "prayer closet," her face was filled with such light and glory that the minister said he knew immediately why her home was so peaceful, a haven of strength and light, and why her elder daughter was a missionary and her two sons were in the ministry. Billy Sunday added his comment, "All hell cannot tear a boy or girl away from a praying mother."

Remember to pray these things for your child:

- physical, emotional, and spiritual health
- an abiding sense of safety and security
- courage to face the problems of each day
- a calm spirit to hear the voice of the Lord
- a willingness to obey
- a clear mind, both to learn and to recall
- a generous spirit toward family and friends
- wise teachers, mentors, and counselors
- unshakable self-worth and personal dignity
- eternal salvation and a home in heaven one day.

> **You are** never so high as when you are on your knees.
> JEAN HODGES

Humble yourselves in the sight of the Lord, and he shall lift you up.

JAMES 4:10 KJV

#1 Pray for your children each day, specifically, and with Scripture and Prayers such as these, from *The Book of Common Prayer*.

• For the Care of Children
#2 Almighty God, Heavenly Father, You have blessed us with the joy and care of children: Give us calm strength and patient wisdom as we bring them up, that we may teach them to love whatever is just and true and good, following the example of our Savior Jesus Christ. Amen.

#3 **• For Young Persons**
God our Father, You see Your children growing up in an unsteady and confusing world: Show them that Your ways give more life than the ways of the world, and that following #4 You is better than chasing after selfish goals. Help them to take failure, not as a measure of their worth, but as a chance for a new start. Give them strength to hold their faith in You, #5 and to keep alive their joy in Your creation; through Jesus Christ our Lord. Amen.

#6

#7

#8

IN HIS CARE

A WOMAN WAS PREPARING to leave her child with a babysitter while she joined her husband for the weekend. He had been out of town for several weeks, and she was looking forward to their time together, even as she felt a little fear and doubt about leaving her four-year-old daughter. She watched from a window as her daughter churned down the driveway on her tricycle, making a right turn at the tree. Her "driving" over the tree roots, however, ended in the tricycle tipping over. She came running into the house with a wail and lifted her skinned knee for her mother to kiss it.

> **A little boy,** age eight, gave a profound definition of parenthood: "Parents are just babysitters for God."

"Who will kiss my knee while you're away?" her daughter asked, her chin quivering. The mother was about to mention the babysitter when she heard herself saying, "I know! God will do it." Her daughter beamed, well satisfied with that answer, and immediately headed back to her tricycle.

The mother found her answer reviving her own faith, and she left for her weekend feeling much more positive about leaving her daughter in the Heavenly Father's hands!

I prayed for this child, and the LORD has granted me what I asked of him. So now I give him to the LORD. For his whole life he will be given over to the LORD.

1 SAMUEL 1:27,28

new insights into ageless questions

Q When I leave my children with a sitter, I feel guilty. But when I try to back out, my husband gets frustrated with me. I can't seem to win. What should I do?

It's been said that the best thing parents can do for their children is to show love toward each other. When parents have a good marriage, it provides children with a sense of security and sets a good example they can follow when they begin to have relationships with people of the opposite sex.

Children take so much focus and energy from parents that often communication diminishes and couples lose a sense of themselves as a pair. This is why it's so important to set aside time to get out of your regular environment with your spouse. Go out and do something that doesn't revolve around your children.

Find a good, trustworthy sitter. Make a regular event of swapping kids with a good friend or family member who also has children. That way, you'll each get a night out. Make it a regular part of your life as a couple. Your children will be fine, and better than fine, knowing that you and Dad value one another enough to take time together.

A CHILD'S PERSPECTIVE

A LITTLE BOY SAT ON A curb in front of his house one day, his head cradled in his hands. A friend walked by and said, "Hey, watcha worried about?"

The boy said, "I've been thinking. Dad slaves away at his job so I'll have lots of cool toys and plenty of food and a nice house with a room all my own. He told me last night he's working hard so I can go to college someday if I want to."

"That's causing you to worry?" asked the friend. "Well, that's not all," said the boy. "Mom works hard every day cooking and doing the laundry and taking me places and helping me when I get sick."

"I don't get it," said the friend. "What do you have to worry about? It sounds like your life is just fine!" The little boy said, "I'm worried they might try to escape!"

Children often **hold a marriage together**—by **keeping** their **parents** too **busy** to **quarrel** with each other.

THE SATURDAY EVENING POST

[Jesus said,] "Permit the children to come to Me;

lighten up

A little boy asked his mom how old she was, to which she teasingly replied, "I don't know, son."
"Look in your underwear," the boy advised. "Mine say I'm four to six."

A girl hugged her mom and said, "Mom, you and God are a lot alike."
"Really?" her mom said, mentally polishing her halo. "How's that?"
"You're both OLD," her daughter replied.

. . . for the Kingdom of God belongs to such as these." MARK 10:14 NASB

INVESTMENT IN LEARNING

> EVERY **WORD** AND **DEED** OF A **PARENT** IS A FIBER WOVEN INTO THE **CHARACTER** OF A **CHILD** THAT ULTIMATELY DETERMINES HOW THAT CHILD **FITS** INTO THE FABRIC OF **SOCIETY**.
>
> DAVID WILKERSON

THE LAZY B Ranch—all 260 square miles of it—lies on the New Mexico and Arizona border. Most of it scrub brush, it has been in the Day family since 1881. When Harry and Ada Mae Day had their first child, they traveled 200 miles to El Paso for the delivery. Ada Mae brought her baby girl home to a difficult life. The four-room adobe house had no running water and no electricity. There was no school within driving distance. One would think that with such limited resources, a little girl's intellectual future might be in question. But Harry and Ada Mae were determined to "stitch learning" into their children.

Ada Mae subscribed to metropolitan newspapers and magazines. She read to her child hour after hour. When her daughter was four years old, she began her on the Calvert method of home schooling and she later saw that her daughter went to the best boarding schools possible. One summer, the parents took their children on a car trip to visit all the state capitols west of the Mississippi River. When young Sandra was ready for college, she went to Stanford, then on to law school . . . and eventually, she became the first woman justice to sit on the Supreme Court of the United States of America.

Every day you make an investment into the character of your child. Make BIG investments!

You will be judged on whether or not you are doing what Christ wants you to. So watch what you do and what you think.

JAMES 2:12 TLB

TOP **10** TIPS for Guiding Your Child to Learn

1. HAVE BOOKS EVERYWHERE, ACCESSIBLE TO YOUR CHILDREN, AND LET THEM SEE YOU ENJOY READING.

2. HEAD TO THE LOCAL LIBRARY FOR STORY TIMES OR TO CHECK OUT BOOKS ON TOPICS OF INTEREST.

3. TAKE ADVANTAGE OF EVERYDAY TEACHABLE MOMENTS.

4. ASK YOUR CHILD QUESTIONS, AND ANSWER THEIR QUESTIONS.

5. CHECK OUT LOCAL MUSEUM EXHIBITS AND TALK ABOUT THE ARTIST OR SUBJECTS.

6. GIVE YOUR CHILD THE SPACE TO EXPLORE AND CREATE.

7. ALLOW YOUR CHILD TO HELP OR AT LEAST OBSERVE AS YOU WORK AROUND YOUR HOME.

8. STIR IMAGINATION BY PRETENDING WITH YOUR CHILD AND GIVING HIM OR HER THE MEANS AND SPACE TO PLAY.

9. SET UP TIMES TO PLAY WITH OTHER CHILDREN.

10. BEGIN TO TEACH YOUR CHILD ABOUT GOD.

CONSIDER THIS!

The following parable of Christ illustrates the gap that can easily exist between hearing and understanding. Jesus was teaching a crowd of people and used the parable of the sower to illustrate the way people receive the word of God. Afterward, when He was alone with His disciples, they asked Him about the meaning of the parables.

Jesus says, "The secret of the kingdom of God has been given to you. But to those on the outside everything is said in parables so that, 'they may be ever seeing but never perceiving, and ever hearing but never understanding; otherwise they might turn and be forgiven'" (Mark 4:11 NRSV) (This was a prophecy from Isaiah 6.)

Don't make the mistake of assuming your children are understanding and applying what they learn in church and Sunday school or from you. Many a preacher's child has left the church with lots of knowledge and little faith because no one thought to ensure the words and ritual were met with understanding.

CONVEYING MEANING

The story is told of a lazy boy who went with his mother and aunt on a blueberry-picking hike into the woods. He carried the smallest pail possible. While the others worked hard at picking berries, he lolled about, chasing a butterfly and playing hide-and-seek with a squirrel. Soon it was approaching time to leave. In a panic, he filled his pail mostly with moss and then topped it off with a thin layer of berries, so that the pail looked full of berries. His mother and aunt commended him highly for his effort.

The next morning his mother baked pies, and she made a special "saucer-sized" pie just for the boy. He could hardly wait for it to cool. Blueberry was his favorite! He could see the plump berries oozing through a slit in the crust, and his mouth watered in anticipation. As he sunk his fork into the flaky crust, however, he found . . . mostly moss!

Many people want to experience the fullness of God's promises in their lives, but they are unwilling to do the work that goes along with most of the Bible's promises. Most of God's promises are if-then statements . . . if we do one thing, then God will do another. Our part nearly always comes first!

> **CHILDREN HAVE NEVER BEEN VERY GOOD AT LISTENING TO THEIR ELDERS, BUT THEY HAVE NEVER FAILED TO IMITATE THEM.**
>
> JAMES BALDWIN

You know what kind of persons we proved to be among you for your sake. And you became imitators of us and of the Lord.

1 THESSALONIANS 1:5-6 NRSV

POWER OF PRAYER

When Dwight D. Eisenhower was Supreme Commander of the Allied invasion of Europe during World War II, he was faced with the responsibility of making one of the most far-reaching decisions ever posed to a single man: the decision to change the date of D-Day at the last moment. The consequences of a wrong decision were so overwhelming, in his opinion, that he felt crushed by the weight of the decision before him. Still, he was the Supreme Commander and the only man who could make the decision that would impact millions of lives. He later wrote:

"I knew I did not have the required wisdom. But turned to God. I asked God to give me the wisdom. I yielded myself to Him. I surrendered myself. And He gave me clear guidance. He gave me insight to see what was right, and He endowed me with courage to make my decision. And finally He gave me peace of mind in the knowledge that, having been guided by God to the decision, I could leave the results to Him."

Few decisions you face in life will ever approach the magnitude of the decision General Eisenhower faced. But whatever size problem we face, God wants us to trust Him enough to leave our problem with Him.

THROUGH THE AGES NO NATION HAS HAD A BETTER FRIEND THAN THE MOTHER WHO TAUGHT HER CHILD TO PRAY.

DEVOTE YOURSELVES TO PRAYER, KEEPING ALERT IN IT WITH AN ATTITUDE OF THANKSGIVING.

COLOSSIANS 4:2 NASB

WISE WORDS

In the same way, the Spirit helps us in our weakness. We do not know what we ought to pray for, but the Spirit himself intercedes for us with groans that words cannot express. And he who searches our hearts knows the mind of the Spirit, because the Spirit intercedes for the saints in accordance with God's will.

ROMANS 8:26-27

booklist

read more about it...
communication in marriage

- *Communication: Key to Your Marriage*
  by H. Norman Wright

- *Covenant Marriage: Building Communication and Intimacy*
  by Gary Chapman

- *Rocking the Roles: Building a Win-Win Marriage*
  by Robert Lewis

- *10 Great Dates to Energize Your Marriage*
  by David and Claudia Arp

- *Boundaries in Marriage*
  by Henry Cloud

TWO IS ENOUGH

A COUPLE IN THEIR mid-thirties were deeply in love and eager to be married. They went to their pastor for the premarital counseling required before their wedding. He probed various questions about their personal faith, ability to communicate openly and honestly, their commitment to each other, their understanding of church service, their views on money, and so on. Finally, he said, half asking and half commenting, "I'm sure you are eager to get started on a family?"

> **Familiarity** breeds contempt—and children.
>
> MARK TWAIN

"Oh, yes, we want children," the young woman said. Her fiancé nodded in agreement.

"Then I hope you have a dozen," the pastor responded enthusiastically.

The man laughed and said, "If that's God's will, I'm willing to do my part."

The young woman, however, gulped and remained silent. "Well, actually, sir," she finally said. "I discussed that with the Lord on my thirty-fifth birthday, and we decided that His will is for no more than two."

Let those also who love
Your name be joyful in You
and be in high spirits.

PSALM 5:11 AMP

"A good name is to be CHOSEN rather than great riches."

PROVERBS 22:1 NKJV

A GOOD NAME

The children of a prominent family thought hard and long about what they could give to their father as a present. They finally decided to commission a professional biographer to write a book detailing the family history. In meeting with the biographer, the children gave him numerous documents and anecdotes to weave into the account, as well as scores of photographs. Then one of the children said, "We have one more matter we need to discuss with you—the family's black sheep." In hushed whispers, they told about an uncle who had been convicted of first degree murder and executed in the electric chair.

"No problem," the biographer assured the children, "I can handle this situation so there will be no embarrassment."

"We don't want to lie," said one of the children.

The biographer agreed, "I'll merely say that Uncle Samuel occupied a chair of applied electronics at an important government institution. He was attached to his position by the strongest of ties, and his death came as a real shock."

A good reputation is something that can never be purchased or traded. It can only be acquired by choices rooted in integrity and morality.

Who's Who: Daniel

Daniel was a young man who resolved to live life by a higher standard than what he saw around him. He lived temperately, putting God before himself and his appetites. When he was among many young men from Judah chosen to train for service to King Nebuchadnezzar, he resolved not to "defile himself with the royal food and wine" that had been apportioned for them (Daniel 1:8).

Daniel asked the chief official for permission to forego what most people would have eaten with gusto and to give Daniel and his friends, Shadrach, Meshach, and Abednego—of fiery furnace fame—only vegetables and water. The official agreed to the request—but only if these Judean boys didn't look sickly at the end of ten days. To the contrary, after ten days Daniel and friends were the picture of vibrant health. God gave the four young men extraordinary wisdom; to Daniel, he gave power to interpret visions and dreams.

According to scripture, Daniel was handsome, intelligent, and capable. He could have accomplished much simply by relying on his own intelligence and stamina. Instead, Daniel looked to God. His reputation brought him before kings and into positions of influence throughout the years of his life. The name Daniel will be associated forever with the man who trusted solely in the Lord of Lords and was allowed to glimpse the future.

Trivia

Fun

Did you know that the song, "The Twelve Days of Christmas" was written by a clergyman to teach children about the Bible?

The first day of Christmas—a partridge in a pear tree represents Jesus Christ, the Son of God. These are the symbols for the other eleven days:

2. Turtle Doves—The Old and New Testaments
3. French Hens—Faith, Hope and Charity—the Theological Virtues
4. Calling Birds—the Four Gospels and/or the Four Evangelists
5. Golden Rings—The first Five Books of the Old Testament, the "Pentateuch," which relays the history of man's fall from grace.
6. Geese a-Laying—the six days of Creation
7. Swans a-Swimming—the seven gifts of the Holy Spirit, the seven Sacraments
8. Maids a-Milking—the eight Beatitudes
9. Ladies Dancing—the nine fruits of the Holy Spirit
10. Lords a-Leaping—the Ten Commandments
11. Pipers Piping—the eleven faithful Apostles
12. Drummers Drumming—the twelve points of doctrine in the Apostle's Creed

GIFTS FROM ABOVE

The darn **trouble** with **cleaning** the house
is it **gets dirty** the next day anyway,
so skip a week if you have to.
The **children** are the most **important** thing.

BARBARA BUSH

During the Christmas season, a bubbly four-year-old girl became caught up in the excitement of the season, especially as she saw the number of presents under the tree slowly increasing as Christmas Day approached. Several times during a day, she would pick up various gifts, examine the box closely—shaking it and looking at it from all angles—and then try to guess what was inside the package.

One evening as she picked up a box, its big red bow fell from it. In a burst of inspiration, she picked up the bow and stuck it on top of her head. With a twinkle in her eyes and a smile as bright as the star atop the Christmas tree, she twirled and announced to her parents, "Mommy and Daddy, look at me! I'm a present!"

This little girl's words were more true than she realized. Our children are the most wonderful gifts God has ever given to us. Take time today not only to admire your child's talents and achievements, not only to enjoy your child's personality, but to truly delight in the fact that your child is a present from the Creator to you and your family!

Children are an heritage
of the LORD: and the fruit
of the womb is his reward.

PSALM 127:3 KJV

CONSIDER
THIS!

Jesus valued the innocent sensibility of a child. Not only did He put a high stake on it, but He set a childlike perspective as a model for all Christians to follow. In the book of Matthew, He says, "I tell you the truth, unless you change and become like little children, you will never enter the kingdom of heaven. Therefore, whoever humbles himself like this child is the greatest in the kingdom of heaven" (18:3, 4).

Encourage and honor the earnest simplicity you see in your child. Catch that youthful optimism, and use it as a model for your approach to faith, believing that God can accomplish things that seem insurmountable in your life and in the world around you.

MIGHTY INTENTIONS

Some years ago a boy in a small town in Florida heard that the Russians were our enemies. He began to wonder about the Russian children, finding it hard to believe they were his enemies too. He wrote a short note: "Dear Comrade in Russia, I am seven years old, and I believe that we can live in peace. I want to be your friend, not your enemy. Will you become my friend and write to me?"

He closed the letter "Love and Peace" and signed his name. He then folded the note, put it neatly into an empty bottle, and threw it into an inland lake near his home. Several days later, the bottle and note were retrieved on a nearby beach. A story about the note appeared in a local newspaper, and a wire service picked up the story and sent it nationwide. A group of people from New Hampshire who were taking children to the Soviet Union as ambassadors of peace read the article, contacted the boy and his family, and invited them to go with them. In the end, the little boy, accompanied by his father, traveled to Moscow and became a peacemaker to the Soviet Union!

One boy decided he could make a difference, and he acted on that. When we act with purity of heart, nothing becomes impossible to us—child or adult!

> **CHILDREN ARE GOD'S APOSTLES, DAY BY DAY SENT FORTH TO PREACH OF LOVE AND HOPE AND PEACE.**
>
> JAMES RUSSELL LOWELL

Behold, children are a gift of the LORD.

PSALM 127:3 NASB

A CHILD'S MOST VALUABLE CURRENCY

CHILDREN SPELL "LOVE" . . . T-I-M-E.

DR. ANTHONY P. WITHAM

A FATHER called his young son while out of town on business and asked, "What would you like for me to bring you?" The two-year-old whispered, "Come out clock." The father wasn't sure he had understood him, so he asked his son to repeat his request. Again the boy said, "Come out clock." The man thought this fairly odd, but the next day on his way to the airport, he bought a large toy clock for his son. His son happily opened the present, played with it a few minutes, and then returned to doing what he had done virtually nonstop since his father had walked in the door: tug at his pants leg. The man looked at his wife as if to say, *What's going on? I don't get it.*

At that moment their cuckoo clock began to strike the hour, and, on cue, figurines of a woodcutter and his wife popped out chasing a little boy and girl, then all four retreated into their cottage. The little boy looked up at the clock, then beamed at his father. The mother suddenly understood. "Each time the clock has struck the hour," she explained, "I've been telling our son, 'It's about time for Daddy to come home.' I think he must have been waiting for you to come out of the clock and chase him around the house!" The father promptly did, to glees of laughter!

Children soon learn how precious time is—that's why when a parent gives it to them they feel so loved!

Don't be fools; be wise: make the most of every opportunity you have for doing good.

EPHESIANS 5:16 TLB

TOP **10** TIPS

for Making More Time for Your Kids

1. BE AVAILABLE FOR YOUR KIDS DURING THEIR PRIME TIME LATE IN THE AFTERNOON.

2. TURN OFF THE TV AND TALK.

3. SET BOUNDARIES WHEN IT COMES TO YOUR INVOLVEMENT IN OUTSIDE PROGRAMS OR ACTIVITIES.

4. BLOCK OUT TIMES ON YOUR CALENDAR TO SPEND SPECIFICALLY WITH ONE CHILD, AS YOU WOULD TO SET A DATE WITH A FRIEND.

5. MAKE ONE BIG GROCERY TRIP EVERY MONTH (OR TWO WEEKS) SO YOU'RE NOT SPENDING TIME RUNNING TO THE STORE.

6. TRY TO FIND A GOOD ROUTINE FOR YOUR FAMILY SO THE KIDS KNOW WHEN TO EXPECT THAT YOU WILL BE "AROUND" FOR THEM TO TALK WITH.

7. PLAN FOR FAMILY OUTINGS, WHERE YOU SPEND TIME TOGETHER.

8. ENGAGE YOUR KIDS IN CONVERSATION THAT IS MEANINGFUL TO THEM.

9. SET UP SOME GROUND RULES FOR THE WAY YOU WANT YOUR FAMILY INTERACTION TO WORK.

10. MAKE TIME TO PRAY WITH YOUR FAMILY AND TO SHOW THEM THAT YOU MAKE TIME IN YOUR LIFE FOR YOUR HEAVENLY FATHER.

RESTING IN TRUST

When Penny saw her daughter's scarlet cheeks, she became alarmed instantly. Candi had undergone a liver transplant as an infant, and when Penny rushed Candi to the hospital, her fears were confirmed: the fever signaled a serious infection. Six-year-old Candi would need another liver transplant!

The same day, Candi's best friend Jason also became ill. He, too, had undergone a liver transplant. Penny and Jason's mom, Nancy, spotted each other in a hospital corridor, in the heat of crisis, each unaware of the other's latest problem. Then, the children's surgeon presented Penny with the toughest choice of her life. A liver had been found, and it was suitable for either child. The medical team had assigned the liver to Candi, but now the team felt Jason's need was more urgent. Was Penny willing to give up the liver intended for Candi so Jason might have it? She said yes.

Jason's transplant went smoothly, but after two weeks, no liver had been found for Candi, whose condition was becoming desperate. At what seemed the last moment, a liver was found. Three weeks after the operation, Candi went home. Penny recalls, "I gave Candi's liver to Jason knowing that somehow God would provide for Candi. I thank Him every day!"

> FOR PEACE OF MIND, RESIGN AS GENERAL MANAGER OF THE UNIVERSE.

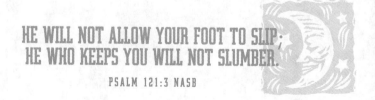

HE WILL NOT ALLOW YOUR FOOT TO SLIP;
HE WHO KEEPS YOU WILL NOT SLUMBER.

PSALM 121:3 NASB

WISE WORDS

I trust in Nature for the stable laws
Of beauty and utility. Spring shall plant
And Autumn garner to the end of time.
I trust in God—the right shall be the right
And other than the wrong, while he endures.
I trust in my own soul, that can perceive
The outward and the inward—Nature's good
And God's.

ROBERT BROWNING

booklist

read more about it...
parenting a strong—willed child

- *Raising Self-Reliant Children in a Self-Indulgent World: Seven Building Blocks for Raising Capable Young People*
  by Stephen Glenn

- *The Happiest Toddler on the Block: The New Way to Stop the Daily Battle of Wills and Raise a Secure and Well-Behaved One- to Four-Year-Old*
  by Harvey Karp, Paula Spencer

- *Parenting with Love and Logic series* (one specifically for Teens)
  by Foster W. Cline, Jim Fay

- *The Strong-Willed Child: Birth Through Adolescence and The New Dare to Discipline*
  by James Dobson

GOOD NEWS, BAD NEWS

AFTER PICKING UP their three-year-old daughter after her first day of nursery school, Rosanna Smith's husband left this message for her on the voice mail system at her office:

Hi, honey. The good news is that Amanda got through her first day at school. The bad news is the principal wants to meet with us.

A second message, recorded awhile later, updated the story:

The good news is that the parents of the boy she bit aren't suing. The bad news is that he had to go to the doctor because of it, and we'll be paying the bill.

Yet a third message, recorded minutes later, added:

The good news is that once we see her teacher, the school will accept Amanda back. The bad news is that Amanda has decided to drop out.

The message ended, "Have a good day!"

A mother once noted that her favorite passage in the Bible was this: "And this too shall pass." It's a good thought to keep in mind when life takes unexpected twists and turns!

> **Do not boast** about tomorrow, for you do not know what a day may bring forth.
> PROVERBS 27:1
> NKJV

A mother is neither cocky, nor proud,

because she knows the school principal may call

at any minute to report that her child has just

driven a motorcycle through the gymnasium.

MARY KAY BLAKELY

THE WORTH OF SOUND WORDS

THROUGH THE YEARS, one of the most popular comic strips about family life was that of "Momma," by Mel Lazarus. Momma was always trying to straighten out her three grown children. Of major concern to her was the proper courtship and marriage of her daughter, Mary Lou.

In one strip, Mary Lou is shown on the front porch saying good night to her boyfriend. He is whispering sweet nothings in her ear. Momma is trying to eavesdrop from the window, but can't quite hear what's going on.

> **A word** aptly spoken is like apples of gold in settings of silver.
>
> PROVERBS 25:11

Once Mary Lou is inside the house, Momma asks, "Mary Lou, what did he whisper to you?" Mary Lou answers, "Ah, just 'love stuff,' Momma."

Momma then says, "Decent 'love stuff' can be spoken freely, out loud. . . . Decent 'love stuff' can be shouted from rooftops." In the final frame of the comic strip Momma's voice crescendos to a climax: "DECENT 'LOVE STUFF' CAN BE EMBROIDERED ON SAMPLERS!"

The **best time** to give **children** your **advice** is when they are **young** enough to **believe** you know what you are talking about.

| new insights into ageless questions

I want more than anything to keep my children from making bad decisions, but when I see what our society promotes for young people, I feel like it's nearly impossible to instill good values. Any suggestions?

It's not impossible to live and speak the right values into your children's lives. It's not easy, either. Just remember that you aren't alone. Parents have been seeking to teach their children to make good choices for thousands of years. Take a look at the book of Proverbs for example. You can almost hear the imploring when the author, presumed to be Solomon, writes: "Listen, my son, to your father's instruction and do not forsake your mother's teaching. They will be a garland to grace your head and a chain to adorn your neck" (1:8-9). Then he says in the next verse, "My son, if sinners entice you, do not give in," and continues to write about the calamitous result of joining the wrong crowd, saying again, "My son, do not go along with them."

Solomon gives plenty of advice to his son about conduct and good judgment, and he always returns to trusting and honoring God as the key to life. Do the same with your children. They may not always listen, but there is value in saying the words, as Solomon did, again and again.

NO SHOTGUN SEAT, THANK YOU

AUTHOR TERESA Bloomingdale writes about driving with her teenager: "The worst 'first' has to be the first time your child drives your car with you sitting beside him. (I do wish they would not call that the 'death seat.') I have tried to avoid this traumatic 'first' by refusing to get into a car with any of my children until they have taken Driver's Education and been duly licensed. But it doesn't help, because if there is anything more nerve-racking than riding with a nervous teenager who is learning to drive, it is riding with a self-confident kid who thinks he knows everything.

"I wish I could say that the more a mother rides with her teenager, the easier it gets to climb into that car, but such is not the case. Every time I get into a car beside one of my driving children, I am convinced that before we travel six blocks we shall both be killed. Thus, whenever possible, I think up an excuse to stay home. . . . I am fully aware that his chances of having an accident will not be decreased by my absence, but since I am sure that he will have an accident with or without me, I would prefer that it be without me. After all, I have nine other children to think of. (And oh, dear God, nine other children who will all be driving someday!)"

> ## lighten up
>
> The thing about parenting is, if you're any good at it, you're working yourself out of a job. And with every new event in your child's life leading him to independence, you're trying to reconcile the two ever-present voices in any mother's mind. One says, "You get out there and make your way in this world, kiddo!" And the other, often overpowering, says, "Oh, honey, you come home with mommy, and I'll make you something nice to eat."
>
> R. MURRAY

Never lend your car to anyone to

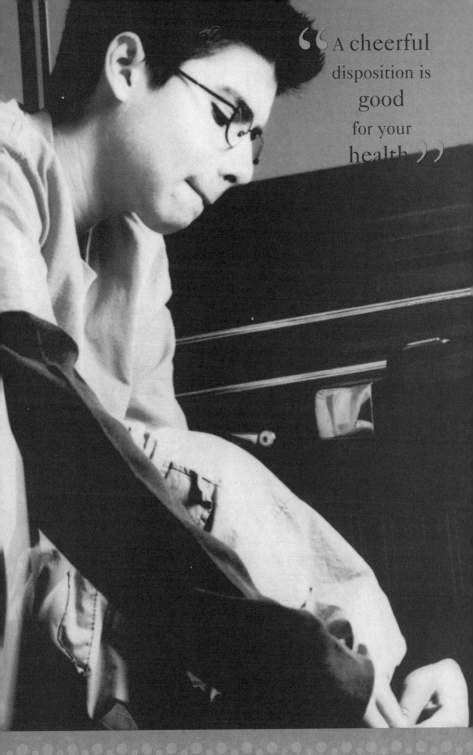

"A cheerful disposition is good for your health"

whom you have given birth. ERMA BOMBECK

A GIFT OF MEMORIES

THE BEST THINGS YOU CAN GIVE CHILDREN, NEXT TO GOOD HABITS, ARE GOOD MEMORIES.

SYDNEY J. HARRIS

THE BED WAS about forty-five years old when Elaine's mother offered it to her. Elaine decided to refinish it for her daughter to use. Then, as she prepared to strip the wood, she noticed that the headboard was full of scratches. She deciphered one scratch as the date her parents were married. Above another date was a name she didn't recognize. A call to her mother revealed the details of a miscarriage before Elaine was born. Elaine suddenly realized the headboard had been something of a diary for her parents! She wrote down all the scratches she could decipher and over lunch with her mother, she heard stories about the times when her mother lost her purse at a department store, a rattlesnake was shot just as it was poised to strike her brother, a man saved her brother's life in Vietnam, her sister nearly died after falling from a swing, a stranger broke up a potential mugging.

Elaine couldn't strip and sand away so many memories—so she moved the headboard into her own bedroom. She and her husband began to carve their own dates and names. "Someday," she says, "we'll tell our daughter the stories from her grandparents' lives and the stories from her parents' lives. And someday the bed will pass on to her."

The memory of the
just is blessed.

PROVERBS 10:7 KJV

TOP **10** TIPS for Safeguarding Memories

1. RECORD THEM WHEN THEY HAPPEN. DON'T WAIT UNTIL DETAILS CAN SLIP FROM YOUR MIND.

2. LABEL PICTURES, IF ONLY WITH NAMES AND DATES.

3. PICK UP A BOOK FORMATTED WITH QUESTIONS AND SPACE FOR RECORDING A PARENT'S MEMORIES.

4. CREATE A MEMORY BOX OR ALBUM FOR EACH CHILD. IT DOESN'T HAVE TO BE FANCY.

5. IF YOU ARE CREATIVE, TURN MEMORABILIA INTO ART.

6. TAKE A SCRAPBOOKING CLASS.

7. MAKE NOTES OF YOUR THOUGHTS IN THE BOOKS YOU READ, INCLUDING YOUR BIBLE.

8. KEEP A PRAYER JOURNAL OR A NOTEBOOK THAT REFLECTS ON YOUR SPIRITUAL JOURNEY OR WAYS GOD HAS WORKED IN YOUR LIFE.

9. TALK WITH YOUR CHILDREN ABOUT YOUR PAST.

10. HELP YOUR CHILDREN TO CREATE SCRAPBOOKS OR JOURNALS OF THEIR OWN.